READER'S DIGEST

FLOWER ARRANGING

READER'S DIGEST

FLOWER ARRANGING

A Complete Course in Selecting and Arranging
Fresh Flowers Throughout The Year

JENNY RAWORTH
& SUSAN BERRY

Photography by MIKE NEWTON

PUBLISHED BY THE READER'S DIGEST ASSOCIATION LIMITED
LONDON • NEW YORK • SYDNEY • CAPE TOWN • MONTREAL

Dedication
To my mother (JR)

First published in the UK in 1996 by
The Reader's Digest Association Limited,
Berkeley Square House,
Berkeley Square,
London W1X 6AB

Conceived, edited, and designed by Collins & Brown Limited

Editorial Director: Sarah Hoggett
Editorial Assistants: Deirdre Mitchell, Corinne Asghar
Art Director: Roger Bristow
Designer: Kevin Williams
Studio photography by Mike Newton

The acknowledgements that appear on page 128 are hereby made
a part of this copyright page.

ISBN 0-276-42235-X

British Library Cataloguing-in-Publication Data
A catalogue record for this book is available from the British
Library.

Printed in Italy

Contents

Introduction 6

Basic Techniques 12
Equipment *14*
Containers *16*
Making Containers *18*
Foundations *20*
Conditioning Flowers *22*
Preparing Flowers *24*
Making a Bouquet *26*
Making a Posy *27*
Ribbons and Bows *28*

Principles of Design 30
Importance of Natural Shapes *32*
Enhancing Flowers *34*
Focus on Foliage *36*
The Effect of Container Shape *38*
Small Container: Seasonal Ideas *40*
Large Containers: Seasonal Ideas *42*

Shape *44*

Flower and Leaf Shapes *46*
Round Arrangements *48*
Facing Arrangements *50*
Round and Low: Spring Hellebore Dish *52*
Round and Dome-shaped: Autumn Centrepiece *56*
Facing Arrangement: Winter Mantelpiece *60*

Colour *64*

Whites and Greens *66*
Yellows and Oranges *68*
Reds and Pinks *70*
Mauves and Blues *72*
Cool Colours: Spring Bowl *74*
Warm Colours: Autumn Basket *78*
Limited Palette: Summer Jug *82*
Clashing Colours: Brilliant Summer Vase *86*

Texture *90*

Textural Effects *92*
Seasonal Textures *94*
Sharp and Spiky: Winter Bucket *96*
Glossy and Matt: Spring Narcissi Pots *100*
Soft and Smooth: Easter Centrepiece *104*

Scent *108*

Scented Plants *110*
Aromatic Herbs *112*
Sweet and Light: Lilac Blossom Pitcher *114*
Strong and Heady: Spring Miscellany *118*
Spicy and Musky: Herb Bowl *122*

Index *126*
Acknowledgements *128*

Introduction

ACH SEASON AFFORDS a wonderfully diverse array of flowers and foliage to the flower arranger, from the first tiny snowdrops of winter to the golden leaves and bright red berries of autumn. Whether you pick flowers for your arrangements fresh from your own garden or buy them from the florist's shop, they contribute a rich source of colour and a focus of interest to any setting – an instant lift to the spirits in any season.

Until recently, the formal art of flower arranging tended to be governed by rules and regulations on shape, form and colour, many of them drawn from Japanese ideas on design. These rules emphasised simplicity, and the flower arrangements that received the most acclaim were often formal creations with a single flower, exquisitely placed. All too often, however, arrangers did not fully understand the underlying design principles, and their results were stiff and contorted combinations of materials and colours that did little to enhance the natural forms of the flowers.

In recent years, flower arrangers have turned to a much more natural style of arranging that tries to mimic the way that plants grow in the garden. It is this approach –

recognizing the natural characteristics of each plant and capitalizing on them – that is at the core of *Flower Arranging*. Concentrate on the main attributes of the plants you use in your arrangements – shape (the sculptured elegance of a lily), colour (the drama of a deep red rose), texture (spiky twigs of dogwood), scent (the heady perfume of lilac). Learn to exploit these attributes and you will soon begin to find it much easier to arrange flowers simply and well.

As with any creative endeavour, you may find yourself so caught up in techniques that you lose sight of what you want to achieve. The key to successful flower arranging lies not so much in physically assembling all the materials as in understanding the characteristics of the flowers you are working with and how different elements come together to make up a successful design. As you master the principles demonstrated in this book, you will gradually become more adept at creating a satisfying and harmonious balance.

RIGHT: *Lisianthus flowers are added to the Queen Anne's lace and lilies seen below, to give variation of texture and shape within the same colour palette. This adds depth and contrast to the arrangement, while maintaining the same overall outline.*

ABOVE: *This simple, delicate arrangement uses only one type of flower (Queen Anne's lace). The foliage forms a collar around the neck of the jug, with the flowers cascading out from the centre.*

ABOVE: *Add another flower – in this case, large, waxy white lilies – and the arrangement becomes more sophisticated-looking, although still simple in mood.*

Sometimes, flowers may provide the starting point for an arrangement and you will need to find a suitable container for them. At other times you may choose the container first, and then select appropriate flowers and foliage for it. Often you will want to create an arrangement for a particular position – a hall table or a low central table in the living room, for example.

Whatever your starting point, you will want to make sure that the elements work well together. Look closely at the textures, as well as the shapes and colours, of both flowers and container. In the following chapters, you will discover important guidelines to choosing wisely.

About this book

Flower Arranging has been organised as a course in the basic principles of flower arranging. After looking at simple flower arranging techniques, such as creating a solid foundation for your arrangements and conditioning flowers so that they last as long as possible, *Flower Arranging* analyses the ingredients of an arrangement – flowers and foliage, container, and so on. The aesthetic elements of flower arrangements – shape, colour, texture and scent – are then examined in detail. Each of these chapters ends with a number of projects based on the principle discussed, giving you a chance to put in practice the things that you have learned. You will find that many of the projects include variations designed specifically to enable you to create a similar-looking display, using a different colour scheme or combination of flowers, at another season of the year.

The aim of *Flower Arranging* is not to provide hard-and-fast rules, but to encourage you to make the most of the material available to you. We have refrained from giving specific varieties in the lists of flowers that make up each project, because you do not need to use exactly the same variety of rose or lavender or clematis and may not be able to find it in your own garden or florist's shop. Once you have grasped the basic principles, you will have the confidence to substitute other flowers of a similar colour, shape or texture.

Fresh flowers may be an ephemeral pleasure, but if you can create one new arrangement each week – even if it is only a tiny bunch of violets in a simple posy bowl – then you and your home will be the richer for it.

RIGHT: *This large winter arrangement would be ideal for a fireplace or free-standing position. It makes use of evergreen foliage and fall berries, relying on contrasts of texture to give it interest. Note how the shape of the arrangement is dictated by the twisted branches that form its framework, giving an asymmetrical form that is entirely natural looking.*

The wealth of material available year round to the flower arranger is, fortunately, very great indeed. Florists are able to supply a remarkable variety throughout the year. By growing your own flowers and foliage, however, you can reduce the cost. Here is a selection of particularly good garden flowers and foliage for flower arranging, organised by season. Unless otherwise stated, it is the flowers that provide the main interest.

Winter
Mahonia sp. – leaves and berries
Holly *(Ilex* sp.*)* – leaves and berries
Ivy *(Hedera* sp.*)* – leaves
Senecio greyii – leaves
Fatsia japonica – leaves and berries
Snowdrops *(Galanthus nivalis)*
Hellebores *(Helleborus* sp.*)*
Viburnum sp. – leaves and berries
Dogwood *(Cornus* sp.*)* – stems
Birch twigs *(Betula* sp.*)*

Spring
Grape hyacinths *(Muscari* sp.*)*
Daffodils *(Narcissi* sp.*)*
Tulips *(Tulipa* sp.*)*
Irises *(Iris* sp.*)*
Freesias *(Freesia* sp.*)*
Buttercups *(Ranunculus* sp.*)**
Primroses *(Polyanthus* sp.*)**
Pansies *(Viola* sp.*)*
Lilac *(Syringa* sp.*)*
Eucalyptus sp. – foliage

* Do not pick from wild without permission

Summer
Delphiniums *(Delphinium* sp.*)*
Stocks *(Matthiola* sp.*)*
Roses *(Rosa* sp.*)*
Peonies *(Paeonia* sp.*)*
Lilies *(Lilium* sp.*)*
Cornflowers *(Centaurea* sp.*)*
Marigolds *(Calendula* sp.*)*
Hosta sp. – leaves
Clematis *(Clematis* sp.*)*
Sweet peas *(Lathyrus odorata)*
Euphorbia sp. – flowers and leaves
Lavender *(Lavandula* sp,*)*
Dill *(Anethum graveolens)* – foliage
Carnations *(Dianthus* sp.*)*

Autumn
Chrysanthemum *(Chrysanthemum* sp.*)*
Achillea sp.
Spiraea sp. – foliage
Honesty *(Lunaria* sp.*)* – seedheads
Pyracantha sp. (berries and leaves)
Nerine *(Nerine bowdenii)*
Gladioli *(Gladiolus* sp.*)*
Michaelmas daisies *(Aster* sp.*)*

RIGHT: *This elegant fan-shaped arrangement consists of carefully chosen, contrasting textures and forms. A limited colour palette – predominantly white, green, and gold – helps to unify the arrangement. The foliage is as important as the flowers in the overall effect.*

Basic Techniques

ALONG WITH PRACTICAL information on the basic equipment you will need for flower arranging, this chapter looks at how to select, prepare and care for flowers and foliage, as well as keep your arrangement in prime condition. Included as well are guidelines for choosing and making containers, and tips on creating suitable foundations for your arrangements. The chapter concludes with ideas for specialist finishing touches to help you achieve a professional-looking result.

Equipment

THERE ARE A NUMBER of essential items of equipment for flower arranging: a pair of strong scissors and a sharp kitchen knife, material in which to anchor flowers and foliage, and various kinds of string, tape and wire to hold arrangements in place. It is also worth keeping raffia and a few ribbons in different colours for finishing touches.

Keep all your equipment in one place for maximum convenience. Work at a bench or a table where you can lay out the flowers and foliage as you work so that they are at hand when you need them. To retain freshness, keep your ingredients in water until you actually need them and work in a reasonably cool environment. You will also need a bin for discarded trimmings.

Fixing equipment
BELOW: *A wide range of tools exists for fixing foundations to containers or flowers to foundations. Wires of different sizes, string, tape and pins are all essential tools.*

Rubber bands

Reel wire

Long pins

Florist's tape

Oasis pins

Florist's wire

Oasis tape

Equipment for cutting
BELOW: *You will need scissors and a knife to cut flower stems. Size and weight are not important, but choose types you feel comfortable handling and make sure they are sharp.*

Knife

Florist's wires

Scissors

Finishing touches
RIGHT: *Ribbons, raffia, rope and string are all useful for decorating containers and for gift wrapping bouquets. Keep a few different styles and colours handy.*

Rope

String

Raffia

Ribbon

Equipment for foundations

BELOW: *You must have a solid foundation for your arrangements so that the flowers stay in the position you have chosen for them. The type of foundation you choose depends on the flower you are using and on your choice of container (see pages 20–21).*

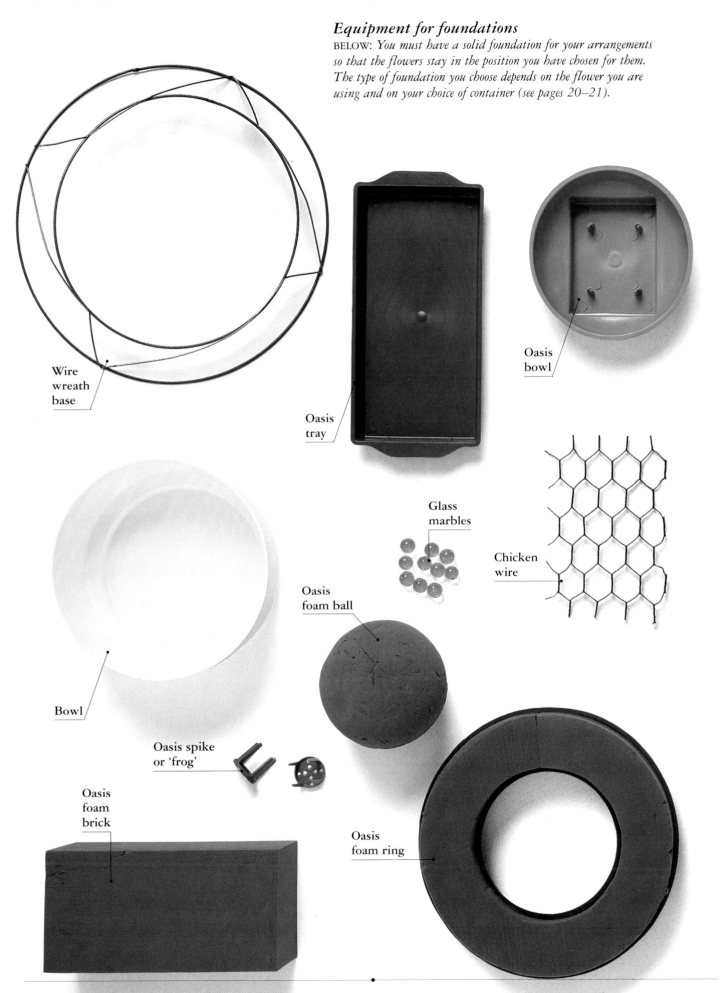

Wire wreath base

Oasis tray

Oasis bowl

Glass marbles

Chicken wire

Oasis foam ball

Bowl

Oasis spike or 'frog'

Oasis foam brick

Oasis foam ring

Containers

YOU CAN USE ALMOST any type of receptacle as a container for a flower arrangement. The important thing is to make sure that the flowers and the container complement each other and that the container does not draw attention away from the flowers.

There are three aspects to choosing a container for your arrangement. First of all, think about the shapes and colours of the flowers you intend to use (see pages 32–33). Then decide whether you want an arrangement that is formal or informal, grand or simple, sophisticated or natural. Finally look at the range of different containers available – glass, china, earthenware, wicker or wooden – and decide which one best suits your flowers and the style of arrangement you hope to create. In making this choice you should think not only about the size and shape of the container, but also about its colour and

texture. The smoothness of glass or china, the coarse surface of terracotta, and the roughness of wicker are each effective with different types of flower. A simple enamel pail, for example, can accommodate wild flowers effectively, while a tall glass vase is ideal for exploiting the glossy beauty of big showy lilies. When in doubt, go for simplicity: plain colours allow the viewer to concentrate on the beauty of the flowers, whereas an elaborately decorated container might compete for attention.

Most people do not have room to keep more than a small collection of containers, but selecting your containers carefully, so that you have as wide a range of shapes, sizes, colours and textures as possible, will allow you to create styles of arrangement to suit any occasion or location. These two pages show a variety of contrasting styles of container, with hints on the sorts of flowers that would look good in them.

China and earthenware containers

BELOW: *Make sure your container combines well with the predominant colour of the flowers in your arrangement. These containers are quite solid looking and would all work nicely with a mass of small, delicate flower heads.*

China jug

Terracotta pot

China jug

China bowl

Wide-necked
glass vase

Wide-necked
glass vase with
crinkly edge

Straight-sided
glass vase

Narrow-necked
glass posy vase

Glass containers

LEFT: *Elegant, cool-looking and sophisticated, glass is best employed for formal arrangements. A plain glass vase makes an especially attractive container for single colour arrangements. Because the stems and contents of the vase are always visible, you should disguise any anchoring material. Glass marbles or an adhesive-tape grid (see page 21) are unobtrusive and convenient materials for anchoring flowers in glassware.*

Decorated china containers

RIGHT: *Decorated china containers combine well with delicate flowers and soft, mixed colours. The container's shape will suggest the best overall form for the arrangement (see pages 38–9), and its colour may either complement or contrast with its contents.*

China rose
bowl

China jug

China mug

Informal-looking containers

BELOW: *Wicker baskets and wooden trugs give a down-to-earth, natural look to an arrangement. Line baskets with plastic to make them waterproof. Enamel pails are perfect for massing small-headed flowers together in an informal arrangement.*

Round plastic-
lined basket

Wooden
trug

Small enamel pail

Plastic-lined
posy basket

Making Containers

PROVIDED THAT YOU clean them thoroughly, you can make your own containers from empty plastic bottles and aluminium cans covered with evergreen leaves or moss. Both evergreen leaves and moss last a long time, and you will be able to use the same container for several arrangements before having to renew the moss or leaf covering.

You can also use recycled containers to make a water-tight inner lining for a non-waterproof receptacle such as a wicker basket or a wooden trug. Baskets and trugs, with flowers heaped inside as if you had just picked them from the garden, are perfect containers for natural-looking, informal arrangements – but without water, of course, the flowers will quickly fade and die. If you are making an inner container, you will not need to cover the whole bottle or can with leaves: a little moss or a collar of leaves around the rim of the inner container will be sufficient to disguise it.

Making a leafy container

This container is made by gluing large evergreen leaves around a cut-down plastic beverage bottle. A green raffia bow provides a natural-looking finish.

1 *Measure the leaves against the bottle. Puncture the bottle at the leaf's tip with the tip of a sharp knife.*

2 *Starting at the puncture point, cut around the bottle using sharp kitchen scissors. Trim the top edge to be level.*

3 *Using all-purpose household glue, attach evergreen leaves to the bottle, placing the stems at the base of the bottle.*

4 *Glue leaves all around the container, overlapping them at the edges.*

5 *Trim the ends of the leaves flush with the container to create a neat edge top and bottom.* INSET: *Tie strands of green raffia around the middle of the container, finishing with a neat bow.*

Leafy-style container
RIGHT: *Glossy leaves transform this bottle into an elegant container.*

Making a mossy container

A beverage can with the top completely removed is covered with
garden moss to create a "grassy" container. The moss will continue to look
attractive even when it dries out and fades in colour.

1 *Make sure the can is watertight and
that there are no sharp edges. Then
glue pieces of moss to the can, covering it as
evenly as possible.*

2 *Continue to add moss until the can is
completely covered. Fill in any gaps
with small pieces of moss.*

3 *Trim around the base and the top of
the can with a sharp pair of scissors to
create a neat, even edge at each end.*

4 *Take 5 or 6 strands of green raffia and, holding one end
firmly in your hand, twist them together to form a thick
rope. Make sure the twists are even and not so tight that the
rope buckles and kinks.*

5 *Tie the raffia rope around the lower part of the moss-covered
container, making sure it lies straight all the way round, and
finish with either a neat knot or a single bow. Trim off any excess
raffia to finish.*

Mossy-style container
ABOVE: *This natural-looking container complements the
informal arrangement of anemones perfectly. The anemones look
almost as if they are growing out of a mossy woodland bank.*

Foundations

BEFORE YOU BEGIN a flower arrangement, you must have a stable base that will hold the flowers in the position you have chosen for them. Sometimes the vase itself provides enough support for the stems, particularly if it has a narrow neck. More often, however, you will need to use a specially constructed foundation, such as wet oasis or chicken wire.

The type of foundation you choose depends both on the type of stems you are using (long, short, stiff, floppy) and on the size and shape of the container. You may also need to fix the foundation itself in position, as it is vital that the foundation does not shift or tip as you insert or move the flowers and stems.

Wet oasis and chicken wire are the most commonly used foundations for flower arrangements, but there are times – when you are using a glass vase, for example – when you need something less mechanical-looking. Clear adhesive tape and glass marbles make effective anchoring materials for such situations (see opposite).

Using wet oasis

Wet oasis is the most common foundation. It is sold in blocks that are soaked in water before the flower stems are inserted. Oasis is not suitable for flowers with very soft stems: the stems may break when you push them into the foundation.

1 *Soak the oasis thoroughly, then cut it with a sharp knife to the size required to fit the container.*

2 *Insert the oasis into the container, if necessary fixing it firmly in place with oasis clips or florist's tape.*

3 *Once the soaked oasis is firmly in position, you can start to make the arrangement.*

Using chicken wire

Chicken wire is a suitable base for both soft-stemmed flowers and large woody stems.

1 *Scrunch the chicken wire into a rough ball shape. Turn the raw edges under.*

2 *Wedge the chicken wire into the container. If necessary, wire it in position (see page 120).*

Solid base
LEFT: *With a base of chicken wire, you can get flowers to stay exactly where you want them – even in a loose, open arrangement.*

Using adhesive tape

In glass containers, any type of foundation will be clearly visible. One solution is to make a clear adhesive-tape grid over the neck of the vase.

 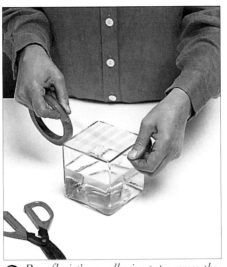 

1 *Fill the vase about two-thirds full with water. Wipe the inside and outside of the neck until it is completely dry.*

2 *Run florist's or adhesive tape across the neck of the vase in a criss-cross grid. Base the size of the holes in the grid on the size of the stems you are planning to use.*

3 *Place the flowers or foliage in the spaces of the taped grid. They will be held upright and in position.*

Using glass marbles

For stiff-stemmed flowers such as lilies, clear glass marbles are a good alternative to an adhesive-tape grid.

1 *Fill a glass container one-third full with clear glass marbles. Pour in fresh cold water until the container is about two-thirds full.*

2 *Push the flowers down into the bed of marbles. Only stiff-stemmed flowers are suitable for this treatment: soft stems will bend when pushed into the marbles.*

Anchored by marbles
LEFT: *The clear glass marbles are almost invisible inside the container. They provide a solid base while allowing attention to remain firmly on the lilies.*

Conditioning Flowers

ALL FLOWER ARRANGERS want their arrangements to last as long as possible. Naturally, some flowers survive longer than others when cut, but there are a number of basic conditioning rules that you should always follow, regardless of the type of flower you are using.

First, of course, make sure that you provide sufficient water. Check the arrangement regularly and be prepared to add fresh water to the container whenever necessary. This is particularly important in very hot weather and in centrally heated environments, where water evaporates as well as being taken up by the flowers. Adding a solution of ammonia and sugar, which you can buy in small packets from florist's shops, to the water also helps to prolong the life of the flowers. You should also make sure that the water in the container is clean. Tainted water (often caused by leaves rotting in the water – see below) causes flowers to droop rapidly.

A moderate, steady temperature is important, too. Never position arrangements close to a radiator or in direct sunlight. You should also avoid moving flowers quickly from a very cool atmosphere to a much warmer one: a sudden change in temperature, such as bringing them from a cool florist's shop into a centrally heated house, can cause them to wilt rapidly. Instead, gradually acclimatise the flowers to higher temperatures by leaving them for a while in a shady porch or entrance hall that is cooler than the rest of the house before you start to make your arrangement.

In addition to the general guidelines outlined above, there are also several ways of conditioning specific types of flower to prolong their life. A variety of stem treatments can be used before you arrange your flowers in order to improve their ability to take up water (see below and opposite). You can also encourage flowers that are still in bud to open out (see opposite).

Removing leaves

Leaves that are left submerged in water soon start to rot. This taints the water and causes the flowers to droop. To prevent this, before you start to create your arrangement, gently strip off any leaves from the lower part of the flower stem that will be below the water line when you have placed the flowers in their container.

Crushing stems

Plants with woody or fibrous stems have difficulty taking up water through their stems. You can aid this process by crushing the last 2.5 cm (1 in) of a plant's stems with a hammer. Roses, in particular, benefit from this treatment.

Removing air locks

To prevent woody-stemmed plants from developing air locks in the stems that prevent them from taking up water, plunge the plant's stems into water that is hand hot for about 20 seconds. INSET: *Remove the stems immediately, plunge them into cold water and leave them in a cool place for 1–2 hours.*

Singeing stems

1 *Flowers such as euphorbia produce milky sap when the stems are cut. This taints the water and deprives the flowers of essential nutrients, causing them to wilt quickly. Check your flowers before you begin an arrangement to see if this is likely to be a problem.*

2 *If it is, use a lit candle or slow-burning match to singe the cut stem briefly. This seals the stem and prevents the sap from seeping out and contaminating the water, while still allowing water to be taken up into the stem.*

Removing dead flower heads

Flowers that have several heads on a stem last longer if you remove the blossoms that have faded. This encourages those flowers that are still in bud to open fully.

Removing stamens

Flowers that have prominent stamens, such as lilies, last longer if the stamens are removed. Pinch them out with your fingers or snip them off with sharp scissors. This technique also reduces pollen and pollen stains.

Preparing Flowers

FOR FLOWERS TO look their best in an arrangement, they sometimes need to be prepared in some way before they are used. Trimming, straightening, de-thorning stems and opening buds are essential techniques to learn. The key to using any of these techniques is to treat the flowers gently: it is all too easy to tear or bruise the petals.

There are many reasons for trimming flowers in flower arranging. You may want to shorten the stems to fit a smaller container. You may want to extend the life of flowers that are slightly past their best by cutting them down in size and placing them in a small bowl. You can make foliage go further by trimming sections of it away from larger pieces or stripping off dying foliage. Use flower heads on stripped stems to bulk up an arrangement of mixed flowers. In all trimming, use a pair of sharp scissors and take care not to damage the stems.

Knowing how to straighten and strengthen stems is a useful way of getting flowers to behave as you want. Stems of flowers that are inclined to bend over – tulips and anemones, for example – can be straightened by wrapping them tightly in paper (see below). Flowers with weak or floppy stems – gerberas, marigolds and anemones – can be stiffened by wiring (see opposite).

When you buy flowers from a florist's shop, you probably look for stems with lots of buds in the hope that they will open out gradually and your arrangement will last longer. Sometimes the buds remain tightly closed, but there are a number of ways of encouraging them to open. Flowers that have several spires of flowers – freesias, gladioli or larkspur, for example – can be dead-headed at the base, allowing the unopened top flower buds to develop. Flowers that have strong, waxy petals – irises, for example – can, if you handle them carefully, be persuaded to open out (see opposite).

Any flowers with thorny stems, such as roses, should be de-thorned before you insert them into oasis. Snipping off the thorns with a pair of sharp scissors is the best way to protect your fingers and prevent you from accidentally bending the stems.

Straightening stems

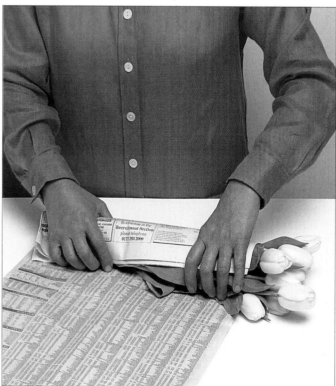

1 *This technique is useful for tulips and anemones, which often have bent or crooked stems. Cut off any faded lower leaves and wrap the stems tightly together in a few sheets of newspaper.*

2 *Place the bundle in a jug or jar of water and leave standing for an hour or two before arranging.*

Wiring stems

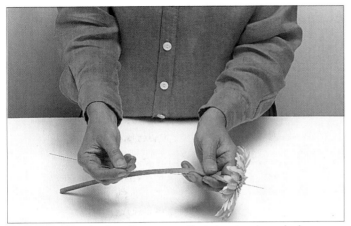

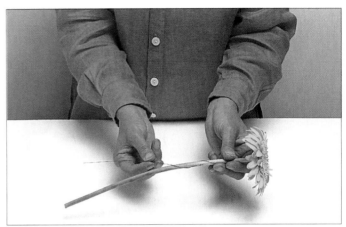

1 *Push a length of medium-gauge florist's wire through the centre of the flower head and out at the base. Leave 5 cm (2 in) of wire protruding out of the head and loop this short end into a hook.*

2 *Hold the wire steady and gently twist the flower stem around it. Trim off any surplus wire. (This technique is suitable for flowers with floppy stems.)*

Removing damaged petals

De-thorning

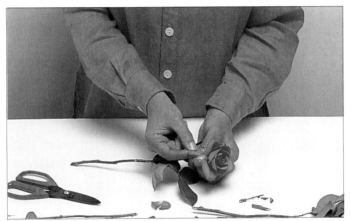

For maximum impact, roses should always be in peak condition. You can improve the look of roses by gently removing any damaged or faded petals before you arrange them.

Thorns make it difficult to insert rose stems into oasis. Strip off any unwanted lower leaves and, using a pair of sharp scissors, carefully snip off any thorns on the lower part of the flower stem.

Making stems less bulky

Opening flower buds

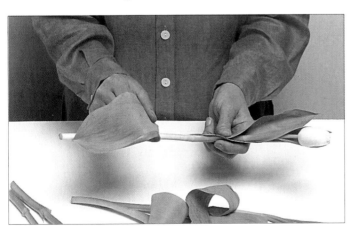

The large number of leaves on tulip stems can make it difficult to display them attractively. Strip off some of the leaves to make the stem less bulky, taking care not to bend the stem as you do so.

Some flowers with strong, waxy petals can be persuaded to open out more fully. Gently pull the petals outwards, using your finger and thumb. Once pulled out, they will stay in position.

Making a Bouquet

THERE ARE MANY OCCASIONS when a bouquet of flowers makes a perfect gift.
The skill lies in arranging the flowers attractively, in tiers, so that the recipient can
see all the flowers at a glance. Placing tissue paper between the tiers helps to
prevent the flower heads from being crushed; it also helps to bulk up
the bouquet, making it look more generous.

1 *Lay out the foliage on a large sheet of cellophane to form a fan-shaped background for the flowers. Trim off any broken or tired-looking leaves.*

2 *Place a collar of tissue paper two-thirds up from the stem end of the foliage. This will raise the flower heads slightly and protect them.*

3 *Start to lay the flowers down, using the tallest first, so that the heads are arranged in tiers down the bouquet.*

4 *Add the rest of the flowers in the shape of a fan (see page 60). Use the shortest stems at the base.*

Presentation bouquet
LEFT: *Fold the cellophane over the flowers and staple the edges together. Twist it around the stems into a "hand hold". Finish with a four-looped bow (see pages 28–9).*

Making a Posy

A POSY MAKES a simple and elegant gift. Whereas a bouquet is generally designed
to be taken apart and rearranged, a posy can be displayed in a vase or jug without any
rearranging. A posy is made up of a series of concentric circles of flowers and foliage.
You only need to make sure that you have enough of each ingredient
to make a complete ring.

1 *To make a posy, work from the centre of the arrangement outwards. Take the central ingredient and make a collar or ring of foliage around it, crossing the stems over each other at the base.*

2 *Add the next ring of flowers slightly below and completely around the first. Cross the stems over each other at the base as in Step 1.*

3 *Add the final rings of flowers and foliage. Tie the posy with string or an elastic band and cover the tie with a ribbon bow (see page 28).*

4 *Trim all the stems to the same length at the base of the posy. This helps the posy to stand upright in a vase. Woody-stemmed flowers are strong enough to stand on their own, supporting the rest of a posy arrangement.*

Versatile posy
LEFT: *The traditional ring design of a posy makes a versatile arrangement that can be hand held or placed in a container.*

Ribbons and Bows

A RIBBON BOW provides a professional-looking finish to a bouquet or posy. Choose a ribbon that complements the flowers: use either a matching or a contrasting colour that picks up at least one of the shades used in the arrangement. Reversible ribbon is the easiest to work with. The steps below show how to make a four-looped bow. A six-looped bow can be made by adding two more loops after Step 3.

1 *Holding the ribbon about 15 cm (6 in) from the end, make the first loop. The long end of the ribbon should lie on top of the 15-cm (6-in) tail.*

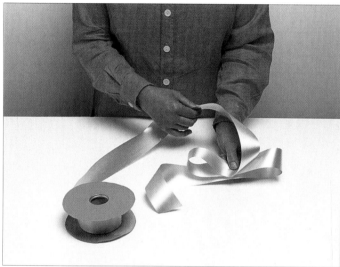

2 *Make a second loop opposite the first, holding the ribbon in the centre with your thumb. Start to make a third loop over the first, bringing the long end of the ribbon back to the centre.*

3 *Make a fourth loop over the second loop, folding the ribbon under towards the back of the bow.*

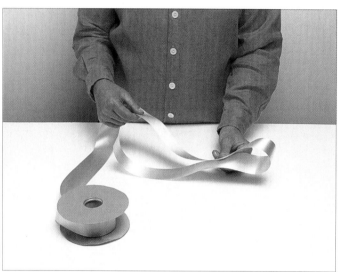

4 *Take the long end of the ribbon under the bow, so that the tail falls smoothly away from the bow.*

5 *Grasp the bow in the centre. Scrunch the centre together with your fingers, fanning out the loops of the bow at the same time so that they are evenly spaced.*

6 *Hold the bow in one hand. Take a piece of medium-grade florist's wire in your other hand and bind it around the centre of the ribbon to hold the loops in place.*

7 *Trim the tails of the ribbon to equal lengths, cutting the ends on the diagonal to make a 'V' shape.*

8 *Tie a narrow piece of the ribbon tightly around the centre of the bow. This covers up the wire that you used in Step 6 to bind the loops in place.*

Four-looped bow
A neatly tied ribbon bow – an easy-to-make and impressive finishing touch for your posies and bouquets.

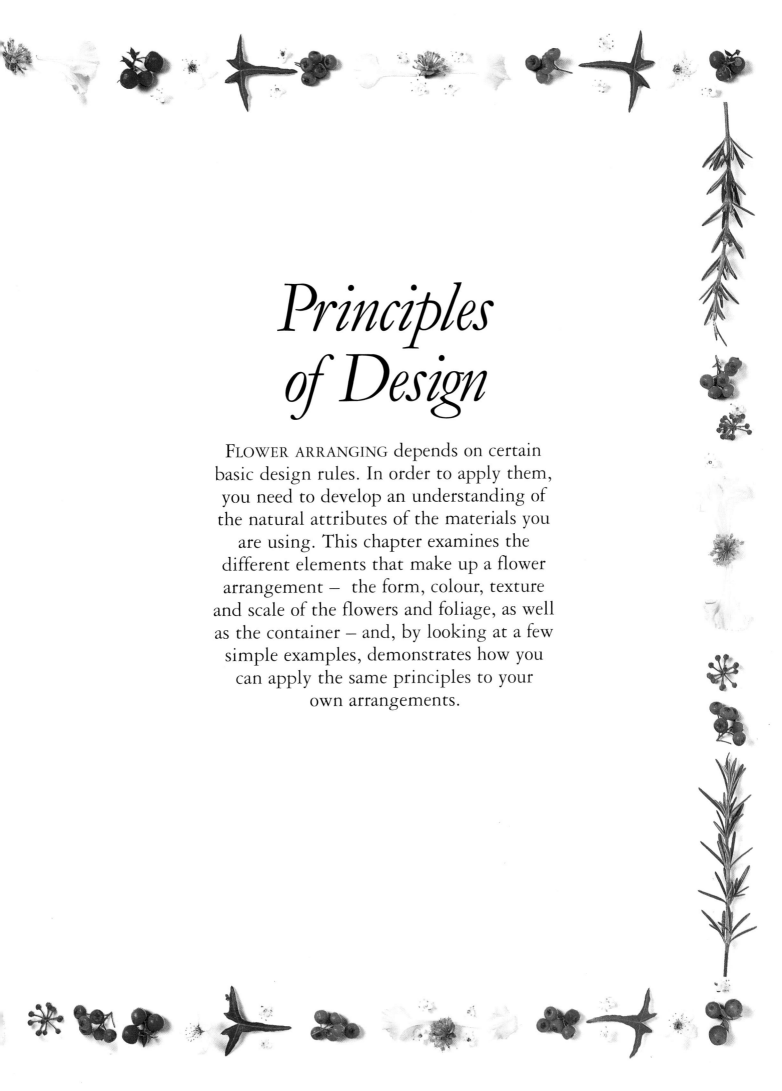

Principles
of Design

FLOWER ARRANGING depends on certain
basic design rules. In order to apply them,
you need to develop an understanding of
the natural attributes of the materials you
are using. This chapter examines the
different elements that make up a flower
arrangement – the form, colour, texture
and scale of the flowers and foliage, as well
as the container – and, by looking at a few
simple examples, demonstrates how you
can apply the same principles to your
own arrangements.

Importance of Natural Shapes

THE SHAPES OF FLOWERS can make just as important a contribution to the overall effect of an arrangement as their colour. Before you start to make an arrangement, analyse the flowers you are using. Are the flower heads large or small, soft or hard, fluffy or waxy? Are the petals wide or narrow, flat or curved? Are the stems straight or twisted, branched or single? Recognising these qualities will help you to decide whether to use the flowers on their own, without any accompaniment, or to arrange them with contrasting forms.

Different flower forms may suggest their own treatment. Large, waxy blooms such as lilies, tulips, daffodils and amaryllis are imposing enough to be used without other flowers. Small, wispy flowers such as cow parsley and campion should be massed together to give them greater impact. Multi-petalled blooms, such as chrysanthemums, roses and carnations, look wonderful grouped together but also work well in mixed arrangements. The three flowers in the arrangements shown here – mimosa, buttercups and tulips – have been arranged to make the most of their natural forms.

Mimosa
(*Acacia dealbata*)

Fluffy spires of mimosa
LEFT: *Golden mimosa requires a simple treatment to set off its soft, delicate appearance. In this arrangement, the fluffy spires are arranged loosely to echo the natural form that mimosa takes on the tree. No further adornment is required.*

Buttercup
(*Ranunculus* sp.)

Dainty buttercups

LEFT: *These buttercups have delicate flower heads and fine stems. Here they are clumped together, almost as if they were still growing in the ground, in a way that echoes their natural growing pattern and heightens the colour impact.*

Tulip leaf (*Tulipa* sp.)

Tulip (*Tulipa* sp.)

Ivy (*Hedera* sp.)

Large, waxy tulips

LEFT: *Tulips have a simple but strongly sculptural form, and the colour is concentrated. Massing them together, with all the flower heads at the same level, creates a bright, eye-catching arrangement.*

Enhancing Flowers

WE TEND TO THINK of flowers as the only element in an arrangement, in part because gift bouquets often arrive with minimal accompanying foliage or a few sprigs of white flowers, such as gypsophila or saponaria. But you often need something extra to set off your flowers in order to create the most appealing effect.

The most important additional element in the flower arranger's repertoire is foliage. While it can stand alone to great effect (see pages 36–7), foliage is more commonly used to set off other elements in a display. When you select foliage to accompany your flowers, think about the colour, shape and texture of the leaves. They should either match the flowers or contrast with them – that is, set them in relief. Flower arranging draws on a wide range of leaf material, from delicate grasslike leaves to large, architectural ones. Small-leaved shrubs, such as spiraea, privet, senecio and leatherleaf, create a densely packed appearance. Finer sword-like leaves such as bear grass, or delicate fronds such as maidenhair fern, give a more ethereal look.

On these two pages, a simple bunch of carnations provides the central element in five different arrangements. In each case, the foliage and accompanying flowers not only change the inherent shapes and character of the display, but also contribute to the overall effect.

The basic ingredient

A single bunch of spray carnations (below) lacks impact on its own, but by combining it with foliage or a few sprigs of white flowers such as saponaria, you can achieve far more interesting effects. The mood of the finished arrangement is dictated by the material you put with the carnations. As you can see, the results vary considerably.

White saponaria
(*Vaccaria hispanica*)

Delicate saponaria

LEFT: *Dainty white saponaria flowers lighten the display, creating a soft, diffuse effect. Their wispiness offsets the more substantial spray carnations, and their own pale flowers harmonise with the carnations, making the arrangement appear less sculptural.*

Spiraea sp.

Alexandrian laurel
(*Danäe racemosa*)

Feathery spiraea
LEFT: *The arching, divided leaves of spiraea soften the display by breaking the rigid outline formed by the carnations. Because the spiraea is slightly darker in tone than the carnations, it creates a subtle contrast.*

Dark-toned Alexandrian laurel
LEFT: *Alexandrian laurel is similar in form to spiraea, but its dark colour creates a more dramatic contrast with the pale carnations.*

Senecio sp.

Privet
(*Ligustrum* sp.)

Rounded senecio
LEFT: *The oval, silvery leaves of senecio match the carnations in intensity of colour and form, creating a well-balanced display. The soft texture, too, matches that of the carnations.*

Glossy privet
LEFT: *Although privet is similar in form to senecio, the texture is glossy. This arrangement has strong colour and textural contrasts, but – like the senecio version – a soft, rounded outline.*

Focus on Foliage

ALTHOUGH FOLIAGE IS most commonly used to supplement flowers, it has all the attributes needed – variety of colour, form and texture – to star as the central element in an arrangement. Foliage colours range from almost grey to bright yellow, blue-green and purple. Leaf sizes and shapes are varied, too, from tiny fronds to large, architectural leaves. Contrasting textures – matt, glossy, spiky, smooth – provide an intriguing element of choice. When planning an arrangement, find an attractive mix of leaf colours, shapes and textures that combines light with dark, small with large and glossy with matt. If you have a garden and want a year-round supply of foliage, you should grow both evergreen and deciduous foliage. The following evergreens are useful: *Viburnum tinus*, *Euonymus* (particularly the variegated form), senecio, rosemary, *Choisya ternata*, ivy (*Hedera* sp.) and holly (*Ilex* sp.). For deciduous leaves grow hostas, astrantias, aquilegia, *Alchemilla mollis* and *Stachys byzantina*. The three arrangements shown here use different sorts of foliage, deciduous and evergreen, with and without flowers, to create very different effects.

Ground elder
(*Aegopodium* sp.)

Viburnum
opulus

Golden rod
(*Solidago* sp.)

Euphorbia polychroma

Hellebore leaf
(**Helleborus** sp.)

Foliage as a frame
LEFT: *In this arrangement of softly contrasting shapes, the collar of deep green hellebore leaves around the neck of the jug provides a frame in which the spires of golden rod and rounded balls of viburnum are set.*

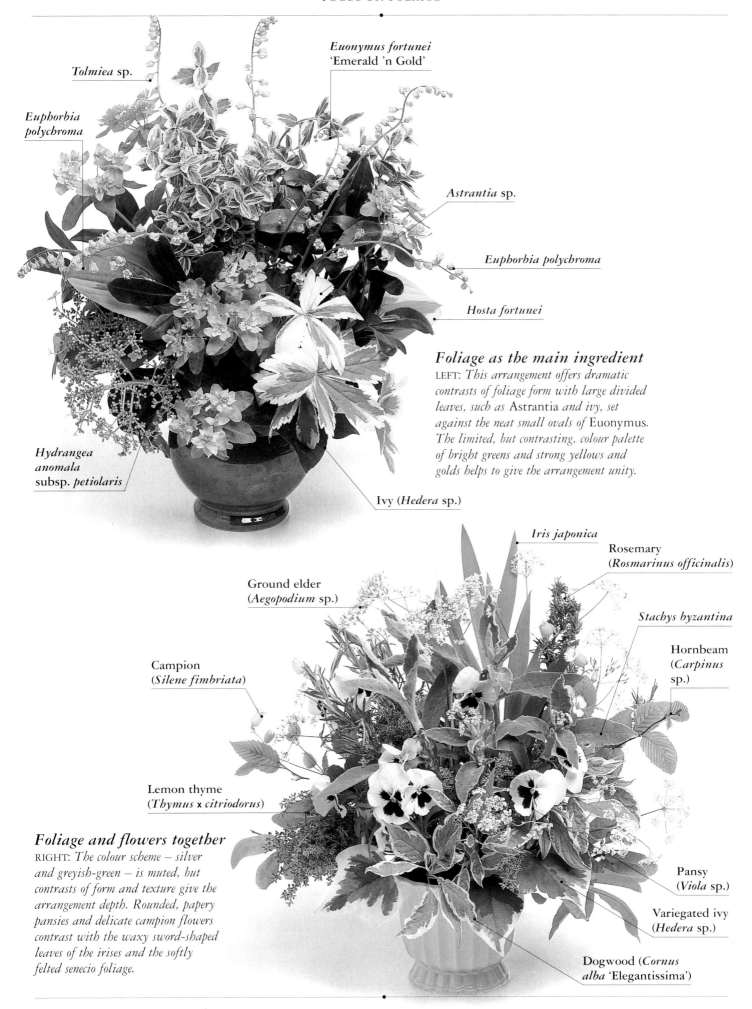

Tolmiea sp.

Euonymus fortunei
'Emerald 'n Gold'

Euphorbia
polychroma

Astrantia sp.

Euphorbia polychroma

Hosta fortunei

Foliage as the main ingredient

LEFT: *This arrangement offers dramatic
contrasts of foliage form with large divided
leaves, such as* Astrantia *and ivy, set
against the neat small ovals of* Euonymus.
*The limited, but contrasting, colour palette
of bright greens and strong yellows and
golds helps to give the arrangement unity.*

Hydrangea
anomala
subsp. *petiolaris*

Ivy (*Hedera* sp.)

Iris japonica

Rosemary
(**Rosmarinus officinalis**)

Ground elder
(*Aegopodium* sp.)

Stachys byzantina

Hornbeam
(*Carpinus*
sp.)

Campion
(*Silene fimbriata*)

Lemon thyme
(*Thymus* x *citriodorus*)

Foliage and flowers together

RIGHT: *The colour scheme – silver
and greyish-green – is muted, but
contrasts of form and texture give the
arrangement depth. Rounded, papery
pansies and delicate campion flowers
contrast with the waxy sword-shaped
leaves of the irises and the softly
felted senecio foliage.*

Pansy
(*Viola* sp.)

Variegated ivy
(*Hedera* sp.)

Dogwood (*Cornus
alba* 'Elegantissima')

The Effect of Container Shape

WHETHER YOU SELECT your flowers to go with a particular container, or choose the container to suit the flowers, your aim should always be to create a display in which flowers and container complement each other. Nothing looks worse than too few stems in an over-large container, or too-tall flowers in a short squat vase.

The key, of course, is proportion. There are no hard-and-fast rules. It is often suggested that in tall arrangements the vase should be one-third of the height of the overall display, but in reality each arrangement needs to be judged on its own merits.

The arrangements on these two pages demonstrate how to display different container shapes and sizes to best advantage, using a simple bunch of chrysanthemums as the starting point. In each case the shape of the container has dictated the finished shape of the arrangement, and the flowers have been treated accordingly: the first display is tall and slender, the second short and squat, and the third low and dome shaped. You can see that by putting a few long-stemmed flowers in a tall, narrow container, or trimming the stems to match the height of a low container and massing the flower heads together in a solid block, you can achieve radically different effects.

Spray chrysanthemum (***Chrysanthemum*** sp.)

Eucalyptus sp.

Tall container, long stems
LEFT: *Tall, narrow containers are ideal for small bunches of long-stemmed flowers because the containers support the stems at the neck, preventing the flowers from splaying sideways. See opposite (below) for what to do when the leaves start to yellow and you need to cut down the stems.*

Spray chrysanthemum
(*Chrysanthemum* sp.)

Wide container, more flowers

LEFT: *For a wide container, increase the number of flowers so that they are massed together in a large, solid block and fill the neck of the container. Cutting all the flower stems to the same height concentrates the colour at one level, with consequent increase of impact.*

Spray chrysanthemum
(*Chrysanthemum* sp.)

Eucalyptus sp.

Shallow bowl, short stems

LEFT: *With a shallow bowl, cut the flower stems short so that the arrangement does not look top heavy. Here the flower heads sit just above the rim. The central stems are slightly longer, giving an attractive domed shape. Low arrangements are useful for flowers that are past their best, since you can cut away yellowing leaves and stems.*

Small Container: Seasonal Ideas

ONE OF THE CHALLENGES faced by anyone who loves to have flowers in the house is finding suitable fresh material for flower arranging all through the year. The trick is to take advantage of whatever is available from season to season. You can create as much effect with a small posy of the first snowdrops in spring, for example, as you can with an elaborate arrangement of summer border flowers. Select what is at its best, and then work out how you can display it to its full advantage.

Using garden flowers and foliage rather than buying material from a florist is a good way to save money. You can replace spring and summer flowers with berries and grasses in autumn, and with twigs, moss and evergreens in winter. Provided that you choose the shapes and the textures as carefully as the colours, even the simplest collection of leaves and berries produces effective results. Evergreen foliage is perenially useful, both for providing a collar of greenery around the rim of the container and as a foundation in which to anchor stems.

As in the demonstration on pages 38–9, look at the shape of your container before you begin and match your choice of flowers and the way you treat them to the container shape and size. Even if you have only a limited supply of containers, you can produce interesting arrangements all through the year. These four seasonal flower arrangements all use the same small round wicker basket, changing the contents to suit the season.

Summer arrangement

RIGHT: *Borders in summer yield an array of flowers in soft colours and varied sizes and shapes. In this small basket, different colours, shapes and textures are massed together to give a tapestry-like effect. The colours harmonise beautifully together.*

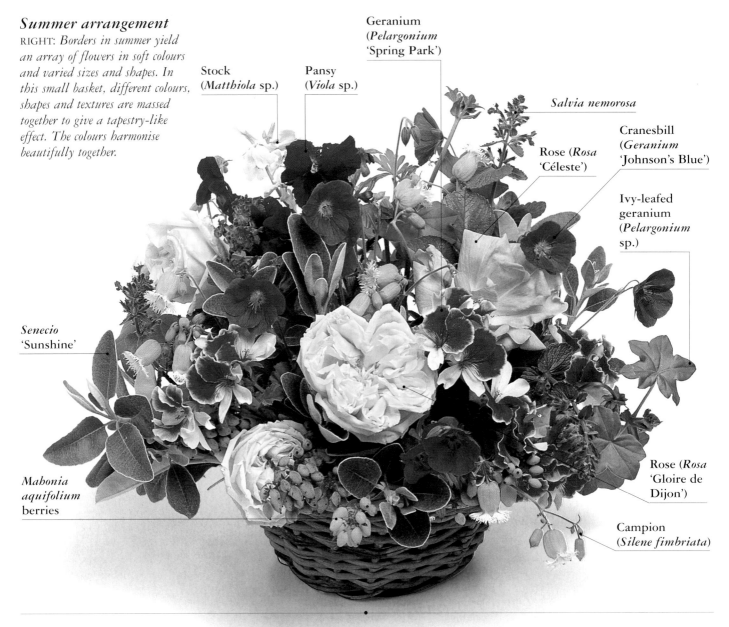

Geranium (*Pelargonium* 'Spring Park')

Stock (*Matthiola* sp.)

Pansy (*Viola* sp.)

Salvia nemorosa

Rose (*Rosa* 'Céleste')

Cranesbill (*Geranium* 'Johnson's Blue')

Ivy-leafed geranium (*Pelargonium* sp.)

Senecio 'Sunshine'

Mahonia aquifolium berries

Rose (*Rosa* 'Gloire de Dijon')

Campion (*Silene fimbriata*)

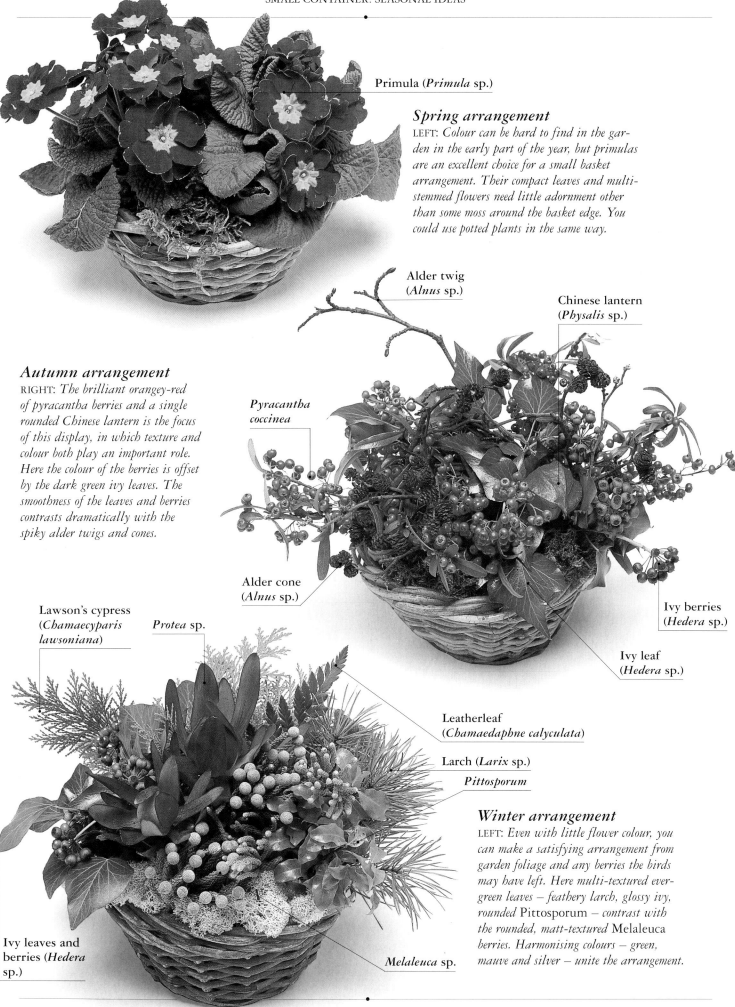

Primula (*Primula* sp.)

Spring arrangement

LEFT: *Colour can be hard to find in the garden in the early part of the year, but primulas are an excellent choice for a small basket arrangement. Their compact leaves and multistemmed flowers need little adornment other than some moss around the basket edge. You could use potted plants in the same way.*

Alder twig
(*Alnus* sp.)

Chinese lantern
(*Physalis* sp.)

Autumn arrangement

RIGHT: *The brilliant orangey-red of pyracantha berries and a single rounded Chinese lantern is the focus of this display, in which texture and colour both play an important role. Here the colour of the berries is offset by the dark green ivy leaves. The smoothness of the leaves and berries contrasts dramatically with the spiky alder twigs and cones.*

Pyracantha coccinea

Alder cone
(*Alnus* sp.)

Ivy berries
(*Hedera* sp.)

Ivy leaf
(*Hedera* sp.)

Lawson's cypress
(*Chamaecyparis lawsoniana*)

Protea sp.

Leatherleaf
(*Chamaedaphne calyculata*)

Larch (*Larix* sp.)

Pittosporum

Winter arrangement

LEFT: *Even with little flower colour, you can make a satisfying arrangement from garden foliage and any berries the birds may have left. Here multi-textured evergreen leaves – feathery larch, glossy ivy, rounded* Pittosporum *– contrast with the rounded, matt-textured* Melaleuca *berries. Harmonising colours – green, mauve and silver – unite the arrangement.*

Ivy leaves and berries (*Hedera* sp.)

Melaleuca sp.

Large Containers: Seasonal Ideas

A LARGE CONTAINER does not have to be crammed full of flowers or filled with large blossoms. As with all types of container, the key to success is to marry the container to the natural shape and style of the flowers (see pages 32–3). A large slender vase, for example, is a perfect receptacle for a tall narrow arrangement of long-stemmed flowers such as lilies, while a deep bowl might be ideal for setting off large, relatively short-stemmed blooms such as hydrangeas. But by its very size, a large container makes an imposing statement. It may be even more important to decide in advance where you are going to position the finished arrangement and make sure that the scale, shape and colours are all appropriate for the setting.

For the two seasonal container ideas shown here – one a large pitcher and basin, the other a large deep tureen – two very different kinds of flowers were used, creating completely different moods and styles. The spring pitcher arrangement is a light and airy-looking composition of delicate, arching wild flowers – ample proof that sprays of tiny flowers can look stunning in a large, chunky container. This arrangement would look superb in an informal, country-style setting. By contrast the summer tureen, in which the flowers in the lower half of the arrangement have been trimmed down in length while those at the top – delphiniumns, antirrhinums and lisianthus – are left untrimmed, is much fuller and denser. This style is more suitable for a structured setting such as a formal dining or drawing room.

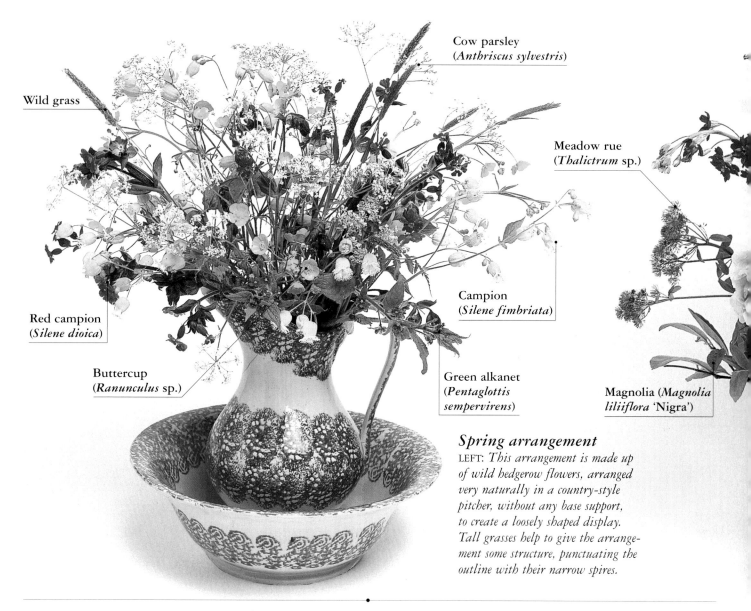

Wild grass

Cow parsley
(*Anthriscus sylvestris*)

Meadow rue
(*Thalictrum* sp.)

Red campion
(*Silene dioica*)

Campion
(*Silene fimbriata*)

Buttercup
(*Ranunculus* sp.)

Green alkanet
(*Pentaglottis
sempervirens*)

Magnolia (*Magnolia
liliiflora* 'Nigra')

Spring arrangement

LEFT: *This arrangement is made up
of wild hedgerow flowers, arranged
very naturally in a country-style
pitcher, without any base support,
to create a loosely shaped display.
Tall grasses help to give the arrangement some structure, punctuating the
outline with their narrow spires.*

Stock
(*Matthiola* sp.)

Delphinium
(*Delphinium* sp.)

Lisianthus
(*Eustoma
grandiflorum*)

Ginger
heliconia
(*Heliconia*
sp.)

Snapdragon
(*Antirrhinum* sp.)

Gerbera
(*Gerbera* sp.)

Summer arrangement
BELOW: *This is a more elaborate display,
with colour and shape carefully balanced
to create a formal appearance. Limiting
the colour palette when using a number
of different flowers helps to give the
composition structure and depth.*

*Trachelium
caeruleum*

Peony
(*Paeonia* sp.)

*Allium
aflatunense*

'Star Gazer' lily
(*Lilium speciosum*
'Star Gazer')

Dogwood
(*Cornus alba*
'Elegantissima')

Rose
(*Rosa* sp.)

*Euonymus
fortunei*
'Emerald 'n
Gold'

Lily
(*Lilium* sp.)

Hosta
(*Hosta* sp.)

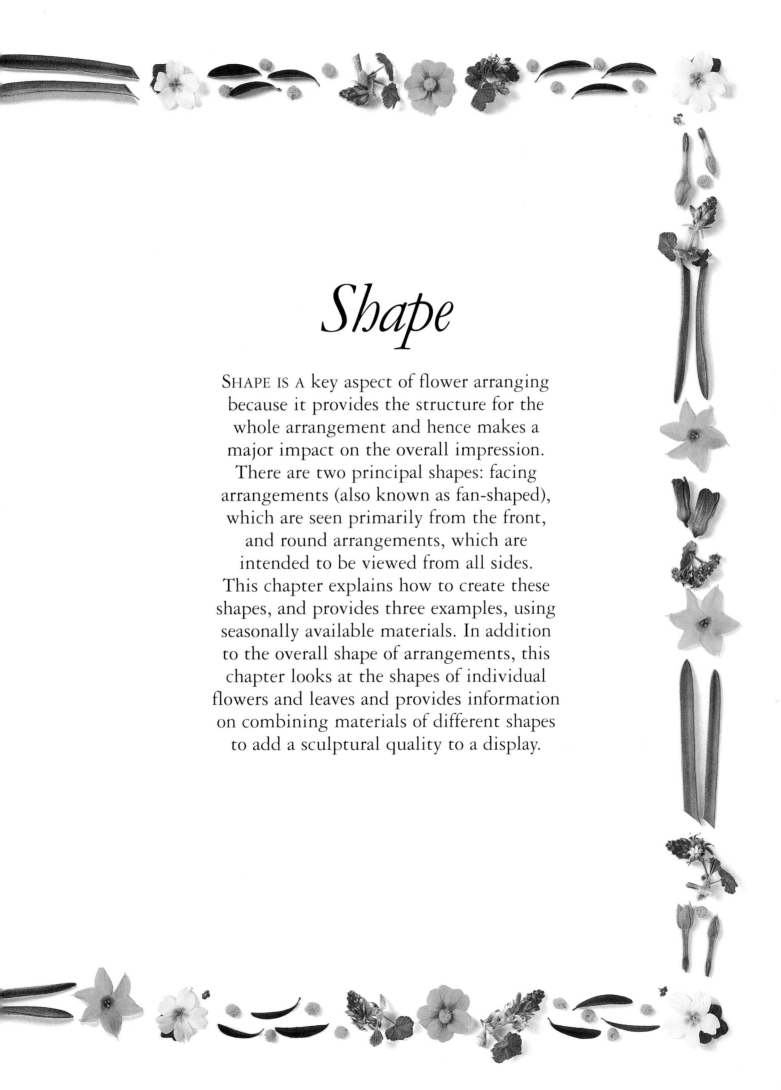

Shape

SHAPE IS A key aspect of flower arranging because it provides the structure for the whole arrangement and hence makes a major impact on the overall impression. There are two principal shapes: facing arrangements (also known as fan-shaped), which are seen primarily from the front, and round arrangements, which are intended to be viewed from all sides. This chapter explains how to create these shapes, and provides three examples, using seasonally available materials. In addition to the overall shape of arrangements, this chapter looks at the shapes of individual flowers and leaves and provides information on combining materials of different shapes to add a sculptural quality to a display.

Flower and Leaf Shapes

FLOWER AND LEAF SHAPES play an important part in flower arranging. In fact, combining different shapes is one of the major factors in creating exciting and unusual flower arrangements. These two pages set out examples of different flower and leaf forms so that you can learn to look at them more closely and analyse for yourself what part they might play in your arrangements.

Soft, fluffy flowers
RIGHT: *Soft, diffuse flower forms – here made up of many individual flowers – can make a useful contrast to more clearly defined flower shapes.*

Lilac
(*Syringa* sp.)

Allium aflatunense

Guelder rose
(*Viburnum opulus*)

Geranium
(*Pelargonium* sp.)

Lisianthus
(*Eustoma grandiflorum*)

Dutch iris
(*Iris* sp.)

Large, waxy petals
RIGHT: *Large, clearly defined, waxy flowers make a bold statement in an arrangement.*

Lily
(*Lilium* sp.)

Lavender
(*Lavandula angustifolia* 'Hidcote')

Rose
(*Rosa* 'New Dawn')

Flower contrasts
RIGHT: *Combining the smooth, soft petals of a rose with hard, small spires of lavender creates an interesting contrast of shape and texture.*

Form without flowers
RIGHT: *Berries and seedheads, too, contribute shape to an arrangement – particularly in autumn and winter when flowers may be in short supply.*

Grape hyacinth (*Muscari* sp.)

Fatsia japonica

Honesty
(*Lunaria annua*)

Clematis
(*Clematis* sp.)

Mahonia
(*Mahonia* sp.)

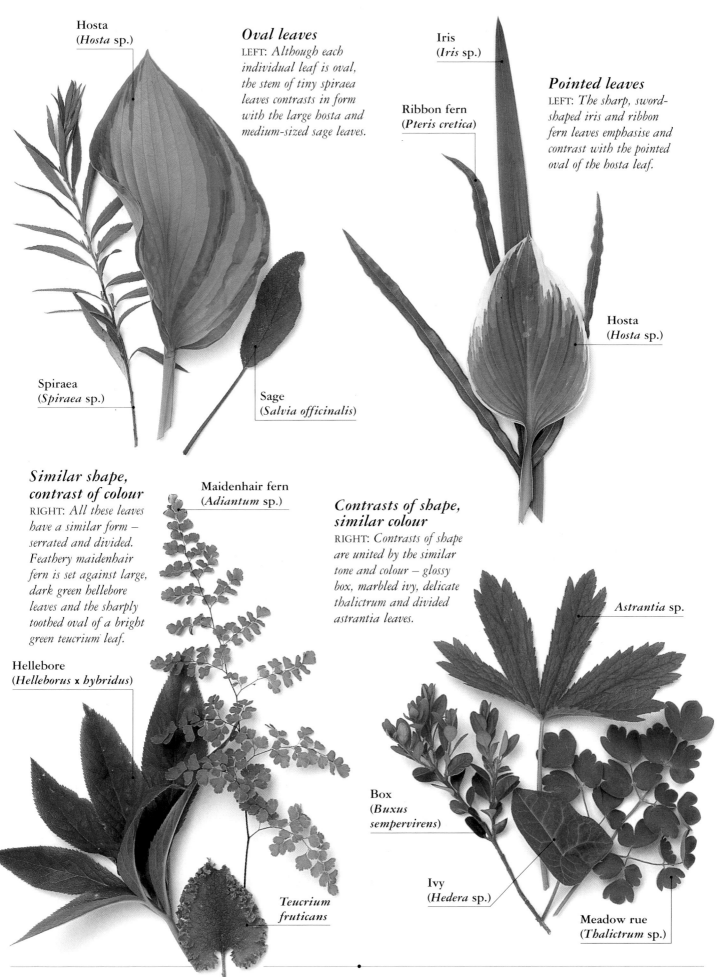

Hosta
(*Hosta* sp.)

Oval leaves
LEFT: *Although each individual leaf is oval, the stem of tiny spiraea leaves contrasts in form with the large hosta and medium-sized sage leaves.*

Iris
(*Iris* sp.)

Pointed leaves
LEFT: *The sharp, sword-shaped iris and ribbon fern leaves emphasise and contrast with the pointed oval of the hosta leaf.*

Ribbon fern
(*Pteris cretica*)

Hosta
(*Hosta* sp.)

Spiraea
(*Spiraea* sp.)

Sage
(*Salvia officinalis*)

Similar shape, contrast of colour
RIGHT: *All these leaves have a similar form – serrated and divided. Feathery maidenhair fern is set against large, dark green hellebore leaves and the sharply toothed oval of a bright green teucrium leaf.*

Maidenhair fern
(*Adiantum* sp.)

Contrasts of shape, similar colour
RIGHT: *Contrasts of shape are united by the similar tone and colour – glossy box, marbled ivy, delicate thalictrum and divided astrantia leaves.*

Astrantia sp.

Hellebore
(*Helleborus* x *hybridus*)

Box
(*Buxus sempervirens*)

Ivy
(*Hedera* sp.)

Teucrium fruticans

Meadow rue
(*Thalictrum* sp.)

Round Arrangements

AN ARRANGEMENT THAT is to be placed in a central position – in the middle of a table, for example – needs to be created in the round so that it looks equally good from all sides. Although the form can vary from a low cluster to a tall dome shape, the aim is always the same: to maintain a balance of flowers and foliage all around, and to leave no obvious gaps or holes.

The most successful round arrangements for central positioning are reasonably symmetrical, but not uniformly rounded. Use a lazy Susan (a revolving turntable) to obtain a good all-round view while you are working. Once the basic shape is established, move the arrangement to its display position, and examine it from different vantage points, as if through the eyes of potential viewers. For example, if you have created a centrepiece for a dinner table, sit down at each place at the table and check that the sides and base of the arrangement, as well as the top, are well covered and have no visible gaps. These two pages show the same round arrangement from different viewpoints and demonstrate that composition and proportion are more important than symmetry.

View from the front

RIGHT: *The overall shape is rounded, but not completely symmetrical. The outer edges are broken by feathery spires of dill foliage which contrast with the waxy, sculptural amaryllis flowers. A collar of senecio foliage softens any suspicion of a hard outline around the neck of the container.*

Dill
(*Anethum graveolens*)

Amaryllis
(*Hippeastrum* sp.)

Guelder rose
(*Viburnum opulus*)

Tulip
(*Tulipa* sp.)

Leptospermum sp.

Rose
(*Rosa* 'Bridal Pink')

Senecio laxifolius

View from the side
LEFT: *From the side, the arrangement appears narrower and taller than from the front, but it still provides a good balance of foliage and flower forms. Note how the flowers extend the same distance from the container on all sides: this prevents the arrangement from looking lopsided.*

View from overhead
RIGHT: *The overhead view is crucial in round arrangements. This arrangement – a harmonious mixture of flowers and foliage in subtly contrasting shades of reds, pinks, greens and whites – looks almost perfectly rounded, with every bloom seen to full advantage.*

Facing Arrangements

THE TRIANGULAR ARRANGEMENT, known to florists as a "facing" or "fan shape," allows an arrangement be placed against a backdrop, such as a wall. Unlike a round arrangement, which is viewed from all sides, a facing arrangement is seen principally from the front. The shape can vary from a very wide fan to a tall and narrow one, but in all cases the flower arranger assembles the display with one primary viewpoint in mind.

Begin by making a skeleton of the shape (usually from foliage) and then fill in this outline with flowers and other material. A facing arrangement does not need even coverage on all sides (the back of the arrangement is never seen once it is in position) and so it requires fewer stems than a round arrangement. But remember that it can occasionally be seen from the sides and make sure that both sides are balanced. Here are three views of one facing arrangement to illustrate the basic construction.

View from the front

RIGHT: *The fan shape is distinct although it has a slightly rounded outline, enhanced by the delicate arching foliage around the edges and base. The long stems of golden rod and stocks, together with variegated euonymus foliage, form the framework of the fan, while yellow freesias and white gerberas fill in the display.*

Golden rod
(**Solidago canadensis**)

Stock
(**Matthiola** sp.)

**Trachelium
caeruleum**

Gerbera
(**Gerbera** sp.)

Freesia
(**Freesia** sp.)

Euonymus fortunei
'Emerald 'n Gold'

Eucalyptus sp.

View from the left side

LEFT: *This side view shows the framework – layers of euonymus, golden rod, and stocks. On this side, gold freesias provide the dominant flower colour.*

View from the right side

RIGHT: *The two sides of a facing arrangement do not need to match each other because they will never be seen at the same time. The full-facing position of the white gerbera at the top of this right side, and the stems of gold freesias below it, produce what is almost another arrangement within the main display.*

Round and Low: Spring Hellebore Dish

MATERIALS

Moss
Round, shallow ceramic dish or bowl
8–10 lettuce leaves (*Lactuca sativa* 'Lollo Rosso')
8–10 heuchera leaves (*Heuchera* 'Palace Purple')
15–20 hellebore flowers and leaves (*Helleborus* x *hybridus*)

THIS STYLE OF ROUND, low arrangement is ideal for a low coffee table, where it can be enjoyed from above. Cup-shaped flowers such as hellebores and anemones work particularly well, as their form complements the shape of the container. You need only a limited number of flowers and a few contrasting leaves for this arrangement. Massing identical flowers together in this way focuses attention on the beauty of the individual blooms, and the use of a single colour also gives the arrangement tremendous impact.

A shallow, round container is ideal for flowers that have weak or floppy stems, since it enables you to make good use of the flower heads alone. Flowers with naturally drooping heads, such as anemones, fritillaries, rose of Sharon flowers or hellebores, will expose their upturned faces to view.

RIGHT: *As this arrangement is designed to be viewed from above, it does not need to be very high. In fact, the flowers are only fractionally higher than the rim of the bowl. Low arrangements like this work best when the flower heads can be seen in their entirety.*

Lettuce
(*Lactuca sativa* 'Lollo Rosso')

Heuchera
(*Heuchera* 'Palace Purple')

Hellebore leaf
(*Helleborus* x *hybridus*)

Moss

Hellebore flower
(*Helleborus* x *hybridus*)

Step-by-step arranging

See also: Importance of natural shapes (pp. 32–3); Flower and leaf shapes
(pp. 46–7); Round arrangements (pp. 48–9); Mauves and blues (pp. 72–3).

1 *Arrange a band of moss approximately 5 cm (2 in) wide around the edge of the tray. In order to disguise the rim completely, make sure the moss extends over the edge.*

2 *In the middle of the tray, place a shallow dish about 3 cm (1½ in) smaller in diameter than the tray and fill it with fresh water.*

3 *Arrange 8–10 lettuce leaves around the edge of the dish, pointing their stems towards the centre. Fill in the spaces between them with heuchera leaves to form a collar.*

4 *Trim the hellebore stalks to about 1 cm (½ in) in length. Arrange the flower heads in the bowl. Include some leaves to give a hint of green in the centre of the arrangement.*

5 *When the centre of the dish is filled with flowers, check the overall appearance. Make sure that none of the flower heads overlap: you may need to adjust the arrangement slightly.*

VARIATION

Make up variations in exactly the same way as the basic design for the Spring Hellebore Dish, anchoring flowers and foliage in a bed of moss. Orchids, ivy and heuchera are used here. Although orchids are expensive, you can get five orchid flower heads – all you need for this project – from a single stem. You could also use spires of large flowers that are past their best – gladioli, for example – by picking off the perfect blossoms and discarding the rest.

Heuchera
(*Heuchera* 'Palace Purple')

Orchid
(*Cymbidium* sp.)

Variegated ivy
(*Hedera* sp.)

Round and Dome-shaped:
Autumn Centrepiece

FLOWERS

5–6 bergenia leaves
(*Bergenia* sp.)

1 bunch muscat grapes

5–6 begonia leaves
(*Begonia* sp.)

4–5 lilies (*Lilium*
'Journey's End')

6–8 nerines (*Nerine bowdenii*)

5–6 lychees

5–6 strawberries

2–3 large red apples

2–3 small red apples

A ROUND, DOME-SHAPED arrangement makes an ideal centrepiece for a dinner table because it can be admired from all sides but is still low enough not to obstruct the view across the table. The key to constructing it is to make it about half as tall in the centre as it is wide. If you raise the arrangement slightly by setting it on a stand, as here, you increase the impact. Work on a lazy Susan that you can turn back and forth in order to check the coverage on all sides. Try not to make the arrangement too symmetrical: here grapes tumble over the edges of the stand, softening the rigid outline.

In this autumn centrepiece, the basic skeleton is created using large begonia and bergenia leaves. Flowers – waxy, exotic-looking lilies and nerines – are inserted to add a strong sculptural element. Finally, fresh fruit, whose gently rounded forms echo the shape of the display, is piled around the base to create a well-rounded shape.

RIGHT: *This arrangement is designed to be seen from all sides. Turn it round to make sure the coverage is even and there are no obvious gaps. Keep the proportions in mind as you work and take care not to make it too high.*

MATERIALS

Small block of pre-soaked oasis

Oasis clip

Oasis fix

Cake stand 23 cm (9 in)
in diameter

Begonia (*Begonia* sp.)

Lily (*Lilium* 'Journey's End')

Small apple

Large apple

Bergenia (*Bergenia* sp.)

Muscat grapes

Lychee

Nerine (*Nerine bowdenii*)

Strawberry

Step-by-step arranging

See also: Importance of natural shapes (pp. 32–3); Focus on foliage (pp. 36–7);
Flower and leaf shapes (pp. 46–7); Round arrangements (pp. 48–9).

1 *Soak the oasis in fresh water (see page 20). Affix the oasis clip off centre on the cake stand with oasis fix. Press the oasis onto the prongs of the oasis clip to secure it.*

2 *Insert the bergenia leaves in a rough triangular shape to form the basic framework (skeleton). Position one leaf in the top of the oasis, and one in the centre of each short side.*

3 *Place the grapes on one side of the arrangement, tumbling them over the side of the stand. Insert the begonia leaves between the bergenia leaves, keeping an overall round shape.*

4 *Hold the lilies against the arrangement to gauge how tall they should be and trim the stalks accordingly. Insert them into the top and sides of the oasis in a rough arch shape.*

VARIATION

*For a fresh-looking summer variation, use seasonal flowers and fruit in
eye-catching shades of green and gold.*

Lily
(*Lilium* sp.)

Hosta
(*Hosta* 'Golden Sunburst')

*Euphorbia
polychroma*

Kiwi fruit

Pear

Ogen melon

5 Fill in any gaps in the overall shape with the nerines.
Distribute the mixed fruit evenly and attractively around the
base of the cake stand beneath the bergenia and begonia leaves.

6 Turn the arrangement to check the overall shape, making sure
there are no gaps or holes. Add more flowers or leaves where
necessary to ensure a balanced shape.

Facing Arrangement: Winter Mantelpiece

MATERIALS

2 oasis clips
Oasis tray
Oasis fix
Block of wet oasis
Florist's tape
6–8 large sprigs magnolia leaves (*Magnolia grandiflora*)
15–20 stems dogwood (*Cornus* sp.)
6–8 large sprigs variegated holly (*Ilex* sp.)
4–5 large sprigs mahonia leaves (*Mahonia* sp.)
12 red roses such as *Rosa* 'Nicole')
6–8 Singapore orchids

Facing arrangements usually have little depth. They are therefore ideal for displaying on narrow shelves or mantelpieces. Foliage provides the skeleton structure for this display. It is then filled out with vivid flowers in lively contrasting colours. Dogwood and orchids around the back and sides soften the rigid outline. This particular arrangement incorporates a number of different textures: soft-petalled roses contrast with jagged holly leaves, and smooth, glossy magnolia foliage offsets twiggy dogwood. Most of these ingredients last a long time, but if the flowers fade before the foliage withers, replace them with something similar.

For a more horizontal fan shape (suitable for displaying on top of a dresser or cupboard), lower the height of the central part of the arrangement and extend the length of the stems at the sides. Make sure the proportions are well balanced: for a low fan shape, the arrangement should be roughly three times as wide as it is tall.

RIGHT: *This arrangement is designed to be seen from the front, so you do not need to worry about the sides and back. Break the outline with twigs of dogwood to prevent the overall fan shape from looking too solid.*

Rose
(*Rosa* 'Nicole')

Singapore orchid

Dogwood
(*Cornus* sp.)

Magnolia grandiflora

Mahonia sp.

Variegated holly
(*Ilex* sp.)

Making the base

Soak the block of oasis for about one hour. Then secure the oasis firmly to the tray to form a stable support for the flowers.

1 *Fix the oasis clips to the oasis tray, securing them with oasis fix. This provides a firm support for the oasis block into which the flowers are inserted.*

2 *Position the pre-soaked oasis on the tray, embedding it in the prongs of the oasis clips. Bind the tray and the oasis firmly together, using florist's tape.*

Step-by-step arranging

See also: Foundations (pp. 20–21); Preparing flowers (pp. 24–5); Focus on foliage (pp. 36–7); Facing arrangements (pp. 50–51).

1 *Insert one magnolia stem into the top of the oasis and two in each side end. Trim the dogwood to twice the length of the magnolia. Place the dogwood at the back to form a fan shape.*

2 *Trim the holly to the same length as the magnolia and insert it into the top and sides of the oasis. Insert a few shorter sprigs of holly at the front.*

VARIATION

*For a summer variation on the mantelpiece arrangement, substitute Easter lilies,
lisianthus, September flowers and campion for the roses and orchids; hosta leaves for the
magnolias; and euphorbia, cotinus and dogwood for the evergreen foliage.*

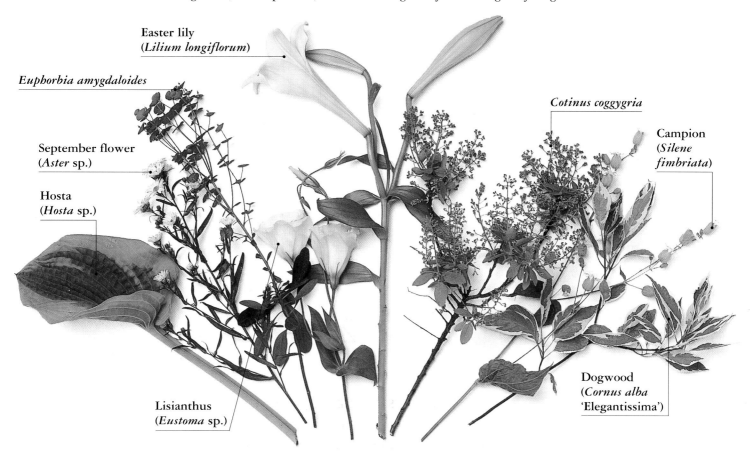

Easter lily
(*Lilium longiflorum*)

Euphorbia amygdaloides

Cotinus coggygria

Campion
(*Silene
fimbriata*)

September flower
(*Aster* sp.)

Hosta
(*Hosta* sp.)

Lisianthus
(*Eustoma* sp.)

Dogwood
(*Cornus alba*
'Elegantissima')

3 *Add the mahonia leaves, spreading them evenly in the centre
and at the sides of the arrangement, following a fan shape.
Insert shorter mahonia stems at the base to soften the lower edge.*

4 *Trim the roses and orchids to approximately the same length.
Place them in the centre and sides of the arrangement, distributing the colours evenly on each side.*

Colour

OF ALL THE attributes of flowers and foliage, colour excites the most attention and makes the most immediate impact. Dark-coloured flowers recede, light colours highlight, and areas of colour intensity or very pale colour produce a compositional focal point. This chapter explains some helpful principles of colour theory and shows how to create interesting and striking colour combinations. It includes a visual reference guide to useful flowers, organized by colour, to enable you to select material for your own colour-based displays.

Whites and Greens

WHITES AND GREENS are the colours of the more retiring flowers and leaves.
They can be used to highlight other materials that have greater depths of colour.
Used on their own, without the addition of other colours, they can produce
striking, near-monochromatic designs. Here is a selection of common
white and green flowers and leaves that are frequently
used in flower arranging.

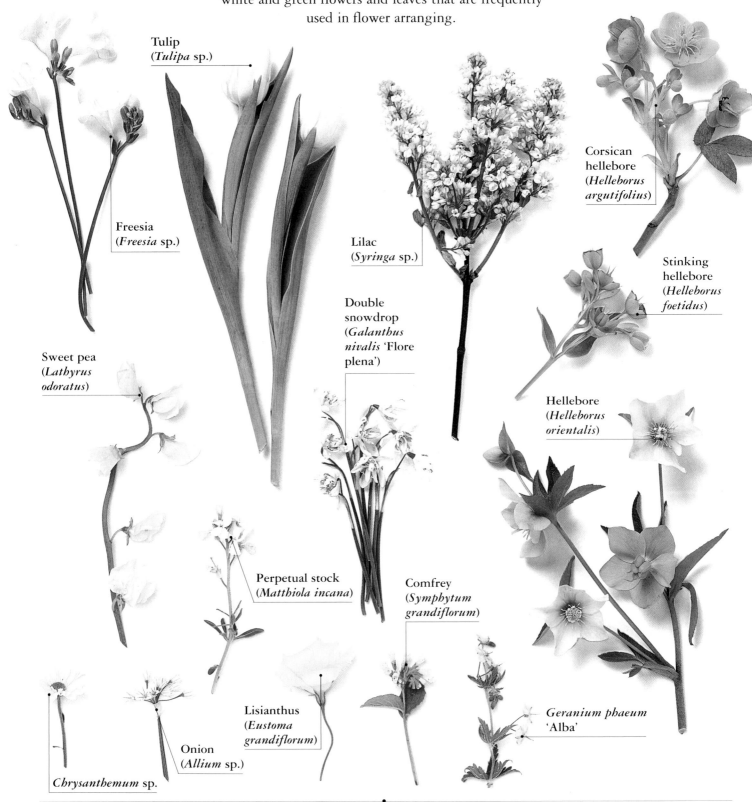

Tulip
(*Tulipa* sp.)

Freesia
(*Freesia* sp.)

Lilac
(*Syringa* sp.)

Corsican
hellebore
(*Helleborus
argutifolius*)

Stinking
hellebore
(*Helleborus
foetidus*)

Double
snowdrop
(*Galanthus
nivalis* 'Flore
plena')

Hellebore
(*Helleborus
orientalis*)

Sweet pea
(*Lathyrus
odoratus*)

Perpetual stock
(*Matthiola incana*)

Comfrey
(*Symphytum
grandiflorum*)

Lisianthus
(*Eustoma
grandiflorum*)

Onion
(*Allium* sp.)

Geranium phaeum
'Alba'

Chrysanthemum sp.

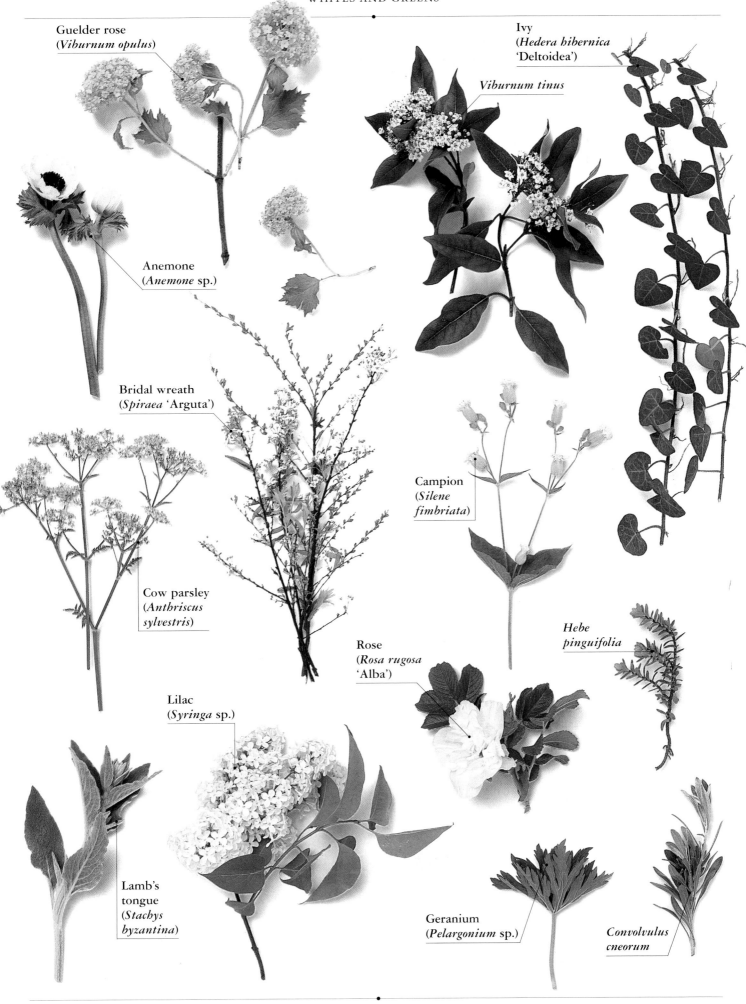

Guelder rose
(*Viburnum opulus*)

Ivy
(*Hedera hibernica*
'Deltoidea')

Viburnum tinus

Anemone
(*Anemone* sp.)

Bridal wreath
(*Spiraea* 'Arguta')

Campion
(*Silene*
fimbriata)

Cow parsley
(*Anthriscus*
sylvestris)

Hebe
pinguifolia

Rose
(*Rosa rugosa*
'Alba')

Lilac
(*Syringa* sp.)

Lamb's
tongue
(*Stachys*
byzantina)

Geranium
(*Pelargonium* sp.)

Convolvulus
cneorum

Yellows and Oranges

YELLOWS AND ORANGES come from the warm end of the colour spectrum. They combine well with blues, and are also effective when used to create strong colour clashes. Use one warm colour only if you prefer a gentle harmonising design – for example, one yellow flower with single or multiple whites and greens. Here is a selection of common yellow and orange flowers used frequently in flower arranging.

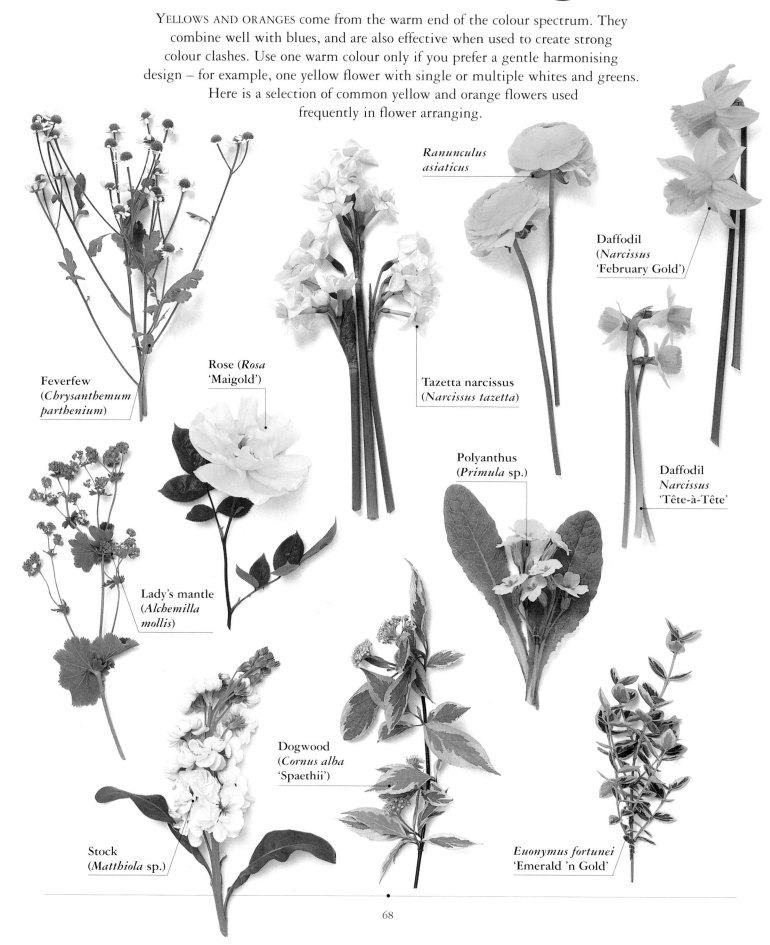

Ranunculus asiaticus

Daffodil (*Narcissus* 'February Gold')

Feverfew (*Chrysanthemum parthenium*)

Rose (*Rosa* 'Maigold')

Tazetta narcissus (*Narcissus tazetta*)

Polyanthus (*Primula* sp.)

Daffodil *Narcissus* 'Tête-à-Tête'

Lady's mantle (*Alchemilla mollis*)

Dogwood (*Cornus alba* 'Spaethii')

Stock (*Matthiola* sp.)

Euonymus fortunei 'Emerald 'n Gold'

Mimosa
(*Acacia* sp.)

Alstroemeria sp.

Mahonia aquifolium

Daylily
(*Hemerocallis* sp.)

Forsythia
(*Forsythia* x
intermedia
'Spectabilis')

Chrysanthemum
(*Chrysanthemum* sp.)

Chrysanthemum
(*Chrysanthemum* sp.)

Lily
(*Lilium* sp.)

Sunflower
(*Helianthus* sp.)

Chrysanthemum
(*Chrysanthemum* sp.)

Carnation
(*Dianthus* sp.)

Florist's rose
(*Rosa* sp.)

Lily
(*Lilium* sp.)

Reds and Pinks

REDS AND PINKS are found in the hottest part of the colour spectrum. Reds and pinks that have some blue in them harmonise well with blue and mauve flowers. Reds and pinks with yellow in them harmonise with yellow flowers. Combinations of bluish-pinks, mauves and white are effective, as are bolder combinations of reds, blues and purples. Here is a selection of common red and pink flowers used frequently in flower arranging.

Singapore orchid

Skimmia japonica

Alstroemeria sp.

Sweet pea (*Lathyrus odoratus*)

Anemone (*Anemone* sp.)

Ranunculus asiaticus

Rose (*Rosa* 'Etoile de Hollande')

Red campion (*Silene dioica*)

Primula (*Primula* 'Captain Blood')

Geranium (*Pelargonium* 'Cascade')

Geranium (*Pelargonium* 'Royal Ascot')

Rosa glauca leaves with chive (*Allium schoenoprasum*) flowers

Hellebore
(*Helleborus hybridus*)

Tulip
(*Tulipa* sp.)

Hyacinth
(*Hyacinthus* sp.)

Lisianthus
(*Eustoma grandiflorum*)

Willow
(*Salix* sp.)

Columbine
(*Aquilegia* sp.)

Columbine
(*Aquilegia* sp.)

Patio rose
(*Rosa de Meaux*)

Camellia
(*Camellia* sp.)

Leptospermum sp.

Geranium
(*Pelargonium* sp.)

Paeony
(*Paeonia* sp.)

Mauves and Blues

MAUVES AND BLUES come from the cool end of the spectrum. On the whole, they are easy to use. They combine well with other colours, either creating contrasts – such as blues with oranges – or harmonies – blues with pinks, for example. The colour blue tends to recede, and the addition of white or pale yellow to an arrangement containing blue boosts contrast and enhances the impact of the blue. Here is a selection of blue and mauve flowers used frequently in flower arranging.

Rosemary
(*Rosmarinus officinalis*)

Polyanthus
(*Primula* sp.)

Lilac
(*Syringa* sp.)

Deadnettle
(*Lamium maculatum*)

Anemone
(*Anemone* sp.)

Sweet pea
(*Lathyrus odoratus*)

Trachelium caeruleum

Clematis
(*Clematis* 'Arabella')

Phlox 'Chatahoochee'

Onion
(*Allium aflatunense*)

Meadow rue
(*Thalictrum* sp.)

Brunnera
macrophylla

Dutch iris
(*Iris* sp.)

Hyacinth
(*Hyacinthus orientalis*)

Bluebell
(*Hyacinthoides
non-scripta*)

Pansy (*Viola* x
wittrockiana)

Delphinium
(*Delphinium
belladonna* 'Blue Bees')

Catmint
(*Nepeta nervosa*)

Cranesbill
(*Geranium*
'Johnson's Blue')

Bugle
(*Ajuga* sp.)

Monkshood
(*Aconitum* sp.)

Catmint
(*Nepeta
faassenii*)

Cool Colours: Spring Bowl

MATERIALS

Chicken wire

Florist's reel wire

Large, shallow china dish

25–30 sprigs *Senecio* 'Sunshine' (leaves only)

3–4 bunches anemones (*Anemone* sp.)

15–20 stems comfrey (*Symphytum grandiflorum*)

10–12 sprigs *Brunnera macrophylla*

ARRANGEMENTS THAT MAKE use of blue colours evoke a mood of peace and restfulness. Here, the coolness comes from the rich blue of anemone flowers, while pale blue brunnera and delicate white comfrey flowers lighten the overall effect. The foliage – silver-grey senecio leaves – provides a delicate foil. Arranged in a china bowl that echoes the flower colours, the effect is refreshing and harmonious.

The use of a restricted colour palette strengthens the overall impact of the arrangement, as does massing the flower heads together at one level, in a single horizontal block. Other flowers that you could use in the cool blue range include ice blue irises, deep blue delphiniums, electric blue cornflowers and pale blue larkspur.

RIGHT: *This round, low arrangement is particularly suitable for displaying anemones because it draws attention to the brilliance of the flower heads, disguising the twisted stems.*

Comfrey
(*Symphytum grandiflorum*)

Brunnera macrophylla

Anemone
(*Anemone* sp.)

Senecio 'Sunshine'

Making the base

A piece of chicken wire forms the base for this arrangement. It is placed inside
the bowl to give a firm support for the flowers and foliage. Oasis may be
substituted for the chicken wire, although this will give a more formal result.

1 *Crumple the chicken wire into a rough
ball. Tuck the raw, jagged edges under-
neath. Place the wire in the china bowl,
pulling up the centre to form a slight dome.*

2 *Anchor the chicken wire in the bowl by
attaching reel wire to one side of the
chicken wire, taking it under the bowl and
securing it on the opposite side.*

3 *Pour fresh cold water into the bowl,
taking care not to overfill it. (Three-
quarters full is ideal.)*

Step-by-step arranging

See also: Foundations (pp. 20–21); Conditioning flowers (pp. 22–3); Importance
of natural shapes (pp. 32–3); The effect of container shape (pp. 38–9); Round
arrangements (pp. 48–9); Mauves and blues (pp. 72–3).

1 *Trim the sprigs of senecio to about
15 cm (6 in) and remove any lower
leaves. Arrange the sprigs around the sides
of the bowl to create a collar of foliage.*

2 *Continue to add the senecio foliage,
arranging it in the centre of the bowl
to give a slight dome shape. The aim is to
form a dense background for the flowers
and to disguise the chicken-wire base.*

3 *Trim the anemones, leaving enough
stalk for them to be able to stand
upright when inserted. Insert the anemones
between the sprigs of senecio foliage. Their
upturned faces should be fully exposed.*

VARIATIONS

If you want to retain the cool colour theme, but don't have access to the flowers shown on page 74, substitute violet-blue pansies and bluebells, backed by apple blossom and the leaves of Mexican orange blossom (below left), or combine blue irises and white tulips with viburnum foliage (below right).

Mexican orange blossom (*Choisya ternata*)

Tulip (*Tulipa* sp.)

Viburnum tinus

Apple blossom (*Malus* sp.)

Pansy (*Viola* sp.)

Bluebell (*Hyacinthoides non-scripta*)

Iris (*Iris* sp.)

4 Continue to add the anemone flowers, creating a balanced display of colour – approximately 24 flower heads are used here.

5 Remove any lower leaves from the comfrey. Gauge the length of the stems by holding them against the arrangement, then trim to size. Add to the bowl, spacing them evenly so they lighten the overall effect.

6 Finally, insert the brunnera flowers in any gaps, in bunches of two or three stems. The brunneras contrast in form and texture with the more dominant anemones, giving the arrangement a soft, airy feel.

Warm Colours: Autumn Basket

MATERIALS

Wet oasis

Wicker basket lined with plastic

12 birch twigs (*Betula* sp.)

Moss

12 large sprigs *Euonymus fortunei* 'Emerald 'n Gold'

2 bunches marigolds (*Calendula* sp.)

2 bunches spray chrysanthemums (*Chrysanthemum* sp.)

RUSSETS, GOLDS, ORANGES, reds and deep pinks form the "hot" section of the colour spectrum and can be used to create a feeling of warmth and welcome. Many late-summer and autumn flowers, including the chrysanthemums and marigolds used in this arrangement, are in colours from the warmer part of the colour spectrum too. Use golden and russet foliage, as well as seasonal berries and fruits, to contribute variety to arrangements that focus on warmth. Most of these warm colours blend happily with each other, but you may lose the overall feeling of warmth if you add pure white or pastel shades to the arrangement.

Containers for warm displays should share some tones with the warm part of the spectrum. Wicker baskets, for example, are ideal, as are earthenware jugs, wooden buckets and terracotta pots. Copper and brass buckets and jugs are also suitable and add a contrasting shiny surface.

RIGHT: A glowing basket of autumn flowers in bronze and russet colours is best placed on a surface that emphasises the warm tones, such as a polished wooden table.

Euonymus fortunei '*Emerald 'n Gold*'

Marigold (*Calendula* sp.)

Moss

Spray chrysanthemum (*Chrysanthemum* sp.)

Making the basket

Tall-handled baskets are widely available, but you can easily make a decorative
handle for any wicker basket from a few birch twigs. Such handles, however,
are not suitable for bearing weight.

1 *Soak the oasis thoroughly. Drain it
and place it in the basket, leaving
2.5 cm (1 in) of oasis above the rim. Make
sure it fits snugly, to create a solid base.*

2 *Bunch half the birch twigs together
and fasten with an elastic band. Insert
the stem ends between the basket and the
oasis. Twist the stems together.*

3 *Repeat Step 2 with the remaining
twigs on the opposite side of the basket
and cross the free ends of twigs over each
other to join in the centre.*

Step-by-step arranging

See also: Containers (pp. 16–17); Focus on foliage (pp. 36–7); The effect of
container shape (pp. 38–9); Yellows and oranges (pp. 68–9).

1 *Cover the edges of the basket with moss, working steadily all
around. This hides the top of the basket and ensures that the
oasis cannot be seen when the arrangement is completed.*

2 *Insert the euonymus foliage around the edge of the basket to
make a framework for the flowers, taking care not to bunch it
too tightly. The gold- and red-tinged foliage will pick up the warm
tones of the marigolds and chrysanthemums.*

VARIATION

To create a similar arrangement in springtime, replace the chrysanthemums with orange-trumpeted daffodils. The creamy-white petals give a slightly lighter and fresher-looking display, but the overall effect is still one of warmth.

Marigold
(*Calendula* sp.)

Euonymus fortunei
'Emerald 'n Gold'

Daffodil
(*Narcissus* sp.)

3 Place euonymus leaves over the moss on the rim. Insert the marigolds into the oasis, the tallest in the centre, the shortest towards the edges.

4 Place the spray chrysanthemums between the marigolds. Place some of the smallest chrysanthemum heads around the sides of the basket.

5 View the arrangement from each of its sides in turn to make sure that the shapes and colours are balanced and that there are no gaps.

Limited Palette: Summer Jug

20-cm (8-in) tall jug

Chicken wire

3–4 *Hosta fortunei* and *Hosta fortunei* 'Aurea Marginata' leaves

3–4 hornbeam (*Carpinus* sp.) leaves

1–2 sprigs *Tolmiea menziesii* leaves and flowers

2 sprigs *Euphorbia polychroma*

2 white clematis flowers such as *Clematis* 'Wada's primrose'

2–3 yellow roses such as *Rosa* 'Maigold'

1–2 heads dill (*Anethum graveolens*)

ONE OF THE BEST ways of giving an arrangement a unified look is to pick a limited palette of colours from the same section of the colour spectrum – say, yellows, greens and blues, or pinks, mauves and blues – and then use deeper and paler shades of these colours to shade from light to dark within the arrangement. This helps to give your arrangement greater substance in much the same way as the use of contrasting textures (see pages 92–5) or flower forms (see pages 46–7). Be careful not to create too great a contrast between light and dark shades, however, or the arrangement will begin to look disjointed. To lighten the overall effect, add white, silver or cream flowers or foliage. Strong colours – bright reds, pinks and oranges, for example – tend to work better in contrasting colour arrangements (see pages 86–9).

RIGHT: *Soft shades of yellow with dark and light greens give a uniformity of colour that is instantly appealing. Touches of white lighten the mood without detracting from the overall colour scheme.*

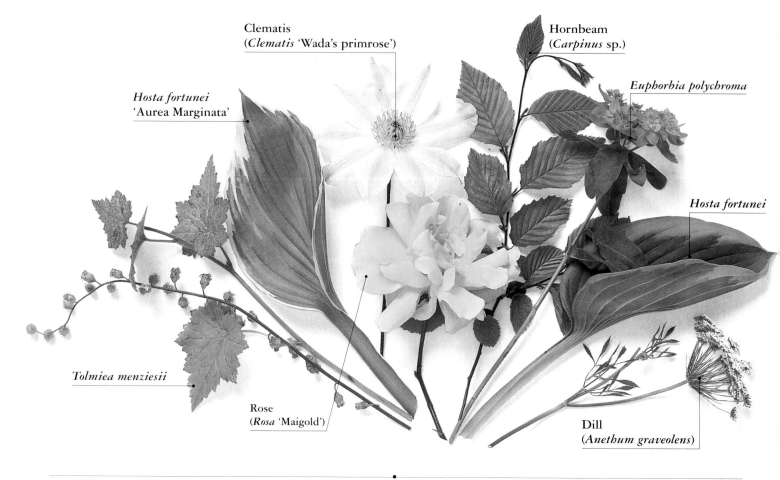

Clematis (***Clematis*** 'Wada's primrose')

Hornbeam (***Carpinus*** sp.)

Euphorbia polychroma

Hosta fortunei 'Aurea Marginata'

Hosta fortunei

Tolmiea menziesii

Rose (*Rosa* 'Maigold')

Dill (*Anethum graveolens*)

Step-by-step arranging

See also: Conditioning flowers (pp. 22–3); Preparing flowers (pp. 24–5);
Importance of natural shapes (pp. 32–3); Focus on foliage (pp. 36–7);
Whites and greens (pp. 66–7).

1 Squeeze the chicken wire into the shape of a ball and insert it into the neck of the jug, pushing it down so that it sits snugly below the rim.

2 Place the hosta and hornbeam leaves around the rim of the jug, distributing them evenly, and fan them out over the edge to make a collar of foliage.

3 Insert the sprigs of tolmiea and euphorbia into the centre of the chicken wire, making sure that they stand higher than the collar of hosta and hornbeam leaves.

4 Crush the stems of the roses (see page 22) and insert. Note that the arrangement is now in various shades of two harmonising colours, yellow and green.

VARIATION

This version is based on the same principle of a limited range of colours, with a slightly deeper colour palette of blues, pinks, mauves and greens.

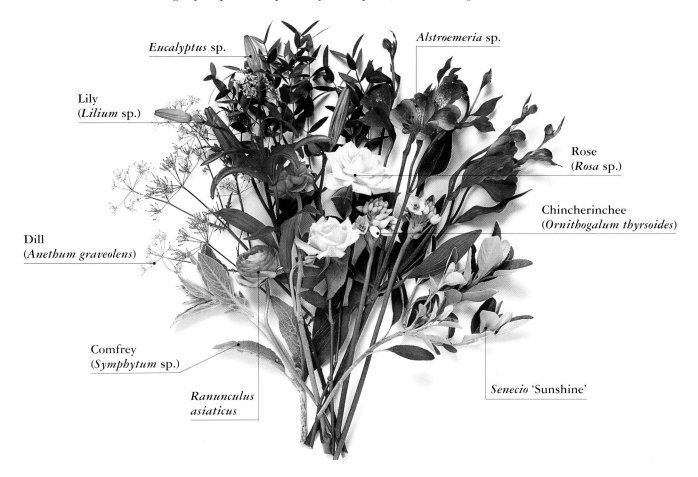

Eucalyptus sp.

Alstroemeria sp.

Lily
(*Lilium* sp.)

Rose
(*Rosa* sp.)

Chincherinchee
(*Ornithogalum thyrsoides*)

Dill
(*Anethum graveolens*)

Comfrey
(*Symphytum* sp.)

Senecio 'Sunshine'

Ranunculus asiaticus

5 *Insert the clematis heads, balancing each one with one of the rose heads already in position. The white of the clematis flowers lightens the overall mood of the arrangement.*

6 *Finally, insert the dill evenly around the arrangement. Note how the greens and yellows, which come from the same part of the colour spectrum, harmonise with each other.*

Clashing Colours:
Brilliant Summer Vase

MATERIALS

15-cm (6-in) square of chicken wire
China pitcher or vase
2 stems orange lilies (*Lilium* sp.)
3 stems scarlet stocks (*Matthiola* sp.)
1 pink paeony (*Paeonia* sp.)
3 large-flowered red roses (*Rosa* sp.)
3 purple columbines (*Aquilegia* sp.)
4 glory lilies (*Gloriosa superba*)
2 orange gerberas (*Gerbera* sp.)
2 yellow marigolds (*Calendula officinalis*)
4 pink roses (*Rosa* sp.)

STRONG, VIBRANT COLOURS can be combined in an arrangement to create an arresting colour clash. For maximum effect, juxtapose several clashing colours – either "hot" colours, such as oranges, pinks and scarlets, or "cool" colours, such as blues and purples. Choose flowers with fairly large heads so the colour looks strong and dense: gerberas, roses, paeonies, lilies, larkspur and stocks, with their large heads or big spires of flowers, are all ideal. To add a contrast of texture and shape and to break up the density of more solid flower forms, use one or two more delicate-looking flowers, such as columbines, freesias or sweet peas.

In this arrangement, florist's and garden flowers have been grouped together for a large, natural-looking display. The pretty blue-and-white pitcher creates the perfect natural shape for the arrangement, its cooler colours setting off the dramatic flowers.

RIGHT: *In this arrangement, fiery reds, burnt oranges and bright pinks combine to create a glowing splash of colour against a sunny yellow wall. The pale pink flowers around the rim of the pitcher form a frame for the arrangement and help to lessen the contrast between the cool blue and white of the container and the vibrant, hot colours of the flowers.*

Columbine
(*Aquilegia* sp.)

Rose
(*Rosa* sp.)

Rose
(*Rosa* sp.)

Marigold
(*Calendula officinalis*)

Rose
(*Rosa* sp.)

Stock
(*Matthiola* sp.)

Lily
(*Lilium* sp.)

Gerbera
(*Gerbera* sp.)

Paeony
(*Paeonia* sp.)

Glory lily
(*Gloriosa superba*)

Step-by-step arranging

See also: Foundations (pp. 20–21); Preparing flowers (pp. 24–5); Importance of natural shapes (pp. 32–3); Yellows and oranges (pp. 68–9); Reds and pinks (pp. 70–71).

1 *Crumple the chicken wire into a ball. Press it into the neck of the pitcher, wedging it in firmly.*

2 *Trim the stems of the largest element of the arrangement, the orange lilies, so that they are roughly twice the height of the container, and insert them at the sides and in the centre.*

3 *Trim the stems of the stocks to roughly the same length as the lilies. Place the stocks near the handle and at the lip of the pitcher, on either side of the lilies.*

4 *Place the paeony in the centre of the arrangement below the lilies and the stocks. Distribute the large-headed red roses evenly around the pitcher, but do not aim for perfect symmetry; the charm of this arrangement lies in its loose, informal style.*

5 *Fill out the sides of the arrangement with the more feathery-looking purple columbines and glory lilies. These flowers help to give height and shape to the arrangement.*

VARIATIONS

*Choose flowers in at least three strong colours for clashing arrangements.
Orange, purple and red (below right) make a bold trio; for slightly more
subtle hues, you could use reds, oranges, mauves and pinks (below left).*

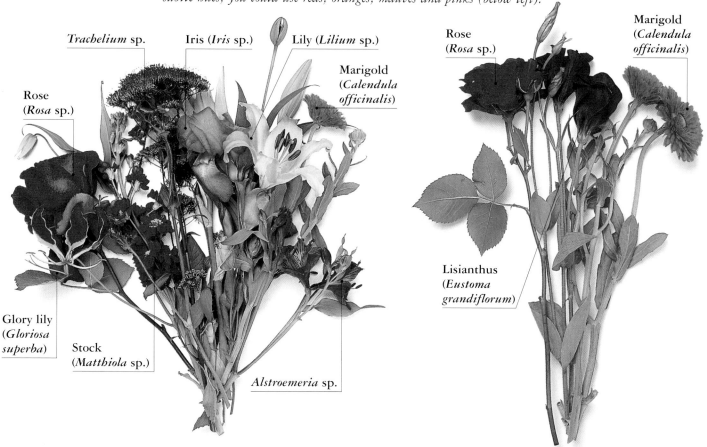

Rose
(*Rosa* sp.)

Trachelium sp.

Iris (*Iris* sp.)

Lily (*Lilium* sp.)

Marigold
(*Calendula
officinalis*)

Rose
(*Rosa* sp.)

Marigold
(*Calendula
officinalis*)

Glory lily
(*Gloriosa
superba*)

Stock
(*Matthiola* sp.)

Alstroemeria sp.

Lisianthus
(*Eustoma
grandiflorum*)

6 *Insert the bright orange gerberas and marigold flower heads among the existing red and pink flowers. This creates the strong clash of colours.*

7 *Add the paler pink roses to contrast with the darker reds and oranges, and to give a more sculptural form to the arrangement.*

8 *Step away from the arrangement and study it. Fill in any holes, and check that the bright colours are balanced throughout the display.*

Texture

TEXTURE, OR THE surface quality of the
materials, contributes a great deal to the
success of an arrangement. Paying special
attention to texture helps to create a feeling
of substance in an arrangement, and
contrasts of different textures, such as
smooth and rough, matt and glossy, add
immeasurably to the final quality. This
chapter illustrates a selection of leaves,
flowers and berries that can be used to add
texture to your arrangements and shows
how to combine them in effective ways.

Textural Effects

WHEN YOU ARE PLANNING an arrangement, consider the texture of the plant material, as well as its form and colour. You can combine similar or contrasting textures, depending on the effect you wish to achieve. Leaves (below) offer the greatest opportunity for textural effects. Use them wherever possible to provide a contrast to the flowers in an arrangement (see opposite).

Ballota sp.

Soft, downy leaves
RIGHT: *Softly felted, downy, or silvery leaves can be used to complement delicate flowers.*

Wild grasses

Lamb's tongue
(*Stachys byzantina*)

Senecio
(*Senecio laxifolius*)

Common fern
(*Polypodium vulgare*)

Divided leaves
RIGHT: *Ferns and slender grasses create a delicate, airy texture in an arrangement.*

Curly mint
(*Mentha spicata* 'Crispii')

Mexican orange
(*Choisya ternata*)

Magnolia
(*Magnolia grandiflora*)

Variegated applemint
(*Mentha suaveolens* 'Variegata')

Ivy
(*Hedera* sp.)

Spiny, slender leaves
RIGHT: *Sharp prickly outlines, slender needles, and pointed ovals are all good foils for larger, softer leaves and flowers.*

Glossy, waxy leaves
RIGHT: *Glossy waxy leaves create an area of dense colour. The glossiness of the surface helps to "lift" the darkness.*

Rose
(*Rosa* sp.)

**Large, waxy flowers –
tiny buds for contrast**
RIGHT: *Waxy tulip heads with
their smooth elongated leaves
make a strong textural contrast
to the rounded heads of
pussy willow.*

Pussy willow
(*Salix* sp.)

Tulip
(*Tulipa* sp.)

Dutch iris
(*Iris* sp.)

Mahonia berries
(*Mahonia* sp.)

**Large, waxy flowers
– gloss and shape
for contrast**
RIGHT: *Smooth, waxy iris
flowers contrast with the
pointed iris leaves, the
divided form of the spires of
mahonia berries and the flat,
glossy leaves of ivy.*

Tree ivy
(*Hedera helix*
'Arborea')

*Ranunculus
asiaticus*

Mexican orange
(*Choisya ternata*)

Fatsia japonica
berries

Bergenia leaf
(*Bergenia* sp.)

Bergenia flower
(*Bergenia* sp.)

Anemone
(*Anemone* sp.)

Skimmia
(*Skimmia rubella*)

**Delicate flowers –
gloss for contrast**
RIGHT: *Papery ranunculus
and delicate pansy flowers
are given a foil of shiny
Mexican orange blossom
leaves and glossy heads of
Fatsia japonica berries.*

Pansy
(*Viola* x *wittrockiana*)

**Delicate flowers –
gloss and size for
contrast**
LEFT: *Big, glossy bergenia and
skimmia leaves, combined with
skimmia buds, make a useful
contrast to the anemones and
bergenia flowers.*

Seasonal Textures

HERE ARE SOME UNUSUAL contrasts of texture for different seasons. It is worth looking for a variety of flower, leaf and berry textures, particularly in winter and spring when there are fewer flowers to choose from. Without textural variations, a flower arrangement can easily look bland and uninteresting.

Skimmia sp.

Rosemary
(**Rosmarinus officinalis**)

Box
(**Buxus sempervirens**)

Mahonia
(**Mahonia** sp.)

Variegated holly
(**Ilex aquifolium**)

Winter and early spring

RIGHT: *Spiky holly leaves and birch catkins contrast dramatically with a florist's Singapore orchid at a time when flowers are in short supply.*

Birch catkin
(**Betula** sp.)

Singapore orchid

Mahonia
(**Mahonia** sp.)

Autumn

RIGHT: *Autumn leaf colours and bright, shiny berries can provide unusual textural contrasts. Here, mahonia leaves and skimmia berries are combined with rosemary and evergreen box.*

Lady's mantle
(**Alchemilla mollis**)

Hazel catkin
(**Corylus** sp.)

Hyacinth
(**Hyacinthus** sp.)

Hebe
(**Hebe** sp.)

Summer

RIGHT: *Feathery heads of lady's mantle give a light, ethereal contrast to the heavy, felted texture of purple sage leaves.*

Purple sage
(**Salvia officinalis** 'Purpurascens')

Skimmia
(**Skimmia rubella**)

Mid-spring

LEFT: *Waxy spires of hyacinths and round skimmia buds contrast with the serrated forms of hazel catkins and hebe leaves.*

Lilac
(*Syringa* sp.)

Eucalyptus sp.

Late spring
LEFT: *Soft, fluffy heads of white lilac are given a foil of waxy eucalyptus leaves.*

Summer
RIGHT: *Tiny divided broom flowers (Genista sp.) are contrasted with the felted, soft and silvery leaves of senecio.*

Broom
(*Genista* sp.)

Senecio
(*Senecio laxifolius*)

Pearl
everlasting
(*Anaphalis* sp.)

Feverfew
(*Chrysanthemum parthenium*)

Summer
RIGHT: *Delicate feverfew flowers contrast with the neat pointed leaves of pearl everlasting.*

Christmas box
(*Sarcocca hookeriana*)

Summer
RIGHT: *Round, waxy camellia leaves and flowers are contrasted with the neatly divided, glossy leaves of Christmas box.*

Camellia
(*Camellia* sp.)

Sharp and Spiky: Winter Bucket

FLOWERS

10–12 branched stems
Lawson's cypress
(*Chamaecyparis lawsoniana*)

2–4 sprays yew
(*Taxus baccata*)

6–8 branched stems holly
(*Ilex* sp.)

2 sprays *Mahonia* sp.

2 sprays *Mahonia* sp.,
sprayed red

8 spray chrysanthemums
(*Chrysanthemum* sp.)

10–12 stems red dogwood
(*Cornus* sp.)

CONTRASTS OF TEXTURE and form help to create the interest in this winter arrangement. The different textures of the leaves and flowers form relatively distinct bands. A tier of soft feathery cypress and yew fronds creates a collar at the rim of the container, surmounted by a fan of spiky mahonia and holly leaves. A central band of soft-petalled flowers provides a striking textural contrast. This in turn is surmounted by the sharp outlines of the slender dogwood stems.

To focus attention on the texture of your arrangement, limit your colour palette to two or three hues. The arrangement shown here combines rich red and deep green for a festive look.

Most gardens in winter have plenty of evergreen foliage. Ivy leaves and berries, conifers, privet and box are among the most common, and you could substitute any of these for the evergreen foliage used in this arrangement.

RIGHT: *Slender dogwood stems, spiky mahonia and holly leaves, soft-petalled chrysanthemums and feathery fronds of cypress and yew create an arrangement with exciting textural contrasts. The overall rounded shape gives an eye-catching focus to the fireplace, and the main colours of red and green produce a warm and festive air.*

MATERIALS

Chicken wire

Large ornamental bucket

Inner container 5 cm (2 in)
smaller in diameter than
the bucket

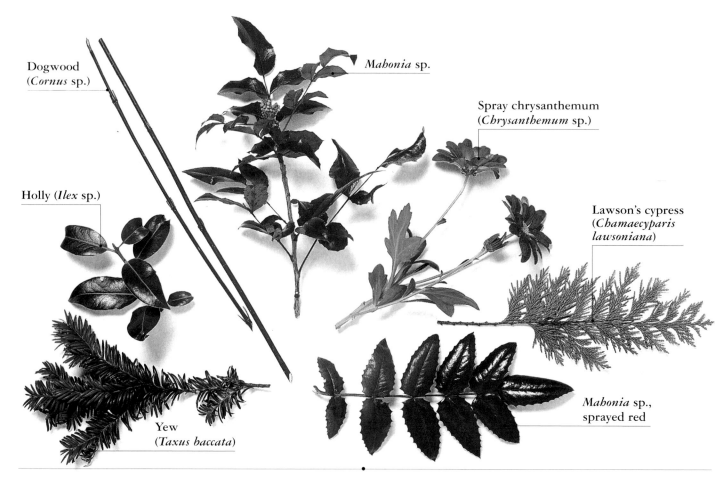

Dogwood
(*Cornus* sp.)

Mahonia sp.

Spray chrysanthemum
(*Chrysanthemum* sp.)

Holly (*Ilex* sp.)

Lawson's cypress
(*Chamaecyparis lawsoniana*)

Yew
(*Taxus baccata*)

Mahonia sp.,
sprayed red

Step-by-step arranging

See also: Foundations (pp. 20–21); Conditioning flowers (pp. 22–3); Focus on foliage (pp. 36–7); Textural effects (pp. 92–3); Seasonal textures (pp. 94–5).

1 *Place a ball of scrunched-up chicken wire in the inner container. Lower the container into the bucket and fill to the three-quarter mark with fresh cold water.*

2 *Trim the cypress stems to 37.5 cm (15 in) and anchor them firmly in the chicken wire around the edges of the container to form a large "collar".*

3 *Trim the yew branches to 50 cm (20 in), and insert them firmly into the wire at the sides of the container.*

4 *Trim the holly to 50 cm (20 in). Insert it around the sides of the container, interspersing it among the yew.*

5 *Place the red and green mahonia in the front and at the sides so that they help to give the arrangement a fan shape.*

VARIATION

A similar version of the arrangement can be made by combining whatever winter foliage you have available with florists' flowers in deep shades of red. Cones provide a strong textural element. Gerberas and long-stemmed anemones provide alternatives for soft- and multi-petalled flowers.

Anemone
(*Anemone* sp.)

Gerbera sp.

Larch stem and cone
(*Larix* sp.)

Variegated holly
(*Ilex* sp.)

Blue pine
(*Abies* sp.)

Variegated ivy flowers
(*Hedera* sp.)

Pine cone
(*Pinus* sp.)

6 *Trim the lower leaves from the chrysanthemums (see page 22) and place the chrysanthemums in a broad band across the centre front of the arrangement.*

7 *Add the dogwood stems to the back of the arrangement. They should be about 25 cm (10 in) higher than the other foliage to break the outline.*

Glossy and Matt:
Spring Narcissi Pots

MATERIALS

Clay pot 15 cm (6 in) tall
Black dustbin liner
Moss
2 bunches small-flowered daffodils (*Narcissus* 'Soleil d'or')

T EXTURE MAY NOT be the first element you notice in the arrangement shown here, but it plays a subtle role in creating the impact. The glossy, waxy flower heads form one block of texture; the simple ribbing of the stems below create the next tier; the rough matt texture of the moss beneath makes a third distinct level; and the smooth, hard surface of the clay pot adds a fourth.

Spring flowers sometimes lack structure in an arrangement, but you can create an effective display by massing the elements together and arranging them texturally in tiers. Alternative spring flowers with a hard, waxy appearance include irises and tulips. For an even simpler version, use summer daisies, or chrysanthemums in autumn.

RIGHT: *Four different textures, arranged in neat horizontal bands, give this arrangement dramatic sculptural impact. As a bonus, it is deliciously scented!*

Small-flowered daffodils
(*Narcissus* 'Soleil d'or')

Moss

Step-by-step arranging

See also: Importance of natural shapes (pp. 32–3); The effect of container shape
(pp. 38–9); Textural effects (pp. 92–3); Seasonal textures (pp. 94–5).

1 *Push a few small pieces of moss into the pot to cover the hole at
the base, or wedge a few broken pieces of oasis into it for the
same purpose.*

2 *Cut a black dustbin liner to 20 cm (8 in) tall, and insert it
into the pot, rolling the edges over the rim. Half fill it with
water. Trim all the narcissus stalks to the same length. The overall
length of stems and flowers should be twice the depth of the pot.*

3 *Place the narcissi in the pot. Insert
moss around the base of the stems to
hold them firmly in position.*

4 *When you are sure that the narcissi are
firmly anchored, fold the edge of the
black plastic over the top of the pot.*

5 *Cover the black plastic with a collar of
moss, making it as smooth and as even
as possible.*

VARIATION

*This very simple arrangement of chrysanthemums in a clay pot gains its impact from
the bands of texture and the simplicity of the colour palette. The flower heads form
one tier of colour and soft texture, the leaves the next and the clay pot the base tier.
Like the pot of narcissi shown on page 101, the effect is very natural and appealing.*

Spray chrysanthemum
(**Chrysanthemum** sp.)

Soft and Smooth: Easter Centrepiece

FLOWERS

18–20 sprigs *Viburnum tinus*
6–8 sprigs *Euonymus fortunei* 'Emerald 'n Gold'
18–20 small-flowered daffodils (*Narcissus* 'Yellow Cheerfulness')
8–10 guelder roses (*Viburnum opulus*)
12 stems *Fatsia japonica* berries
16–18 yellow primroses (*Primula* sp.)
12 purple pansies (*Viola* x *wittrockiana*)
1–2 stems bridal wreath (*Spiraea* 'Arguta')
4–6 sprigs *Brunnera macrophylla*

THE FLOWERS AND LEAVES in this table decoration all have a similar overall texture – soft and smooth. This helps to unify the arrangement – a useful tip for dealing with a large number of different materials. The size of the ingredients is important, too: all the flowers are small in scale and no one element dominates the others. Limiting the colour palette also helps to pull the arrangement together, focusing attention on the tiny speckled quail's eggs in the centre. It is, however, important to include some contrasting elements, and this is achieved by choosing flowers that have different forms (shapes). Here, primroses, pansies and daffodils, with their clearly separated petals, tightly packed heads of guelder roses, round berries of fatsia japonica, and sprigs of tiny bridal wreath and brunnera flowers combine to make an attractive spring centrepiece.

RIGHT: *A range of small-flowered spring plants with smooth petals and soft rounded forms that echo the shape of the container give this arrangement its balance and unity. Glossy, sharp-edged leaves such as holly would look obtrusive and break the neat, rounded outline.*

MATERIALS

35-cm (14-in) wet oasis ring
40-cm (16-in) square of cardboard or aluminium foil
Marker pen and florist's tape
Moss
Chocolate, quails' or painted eggs

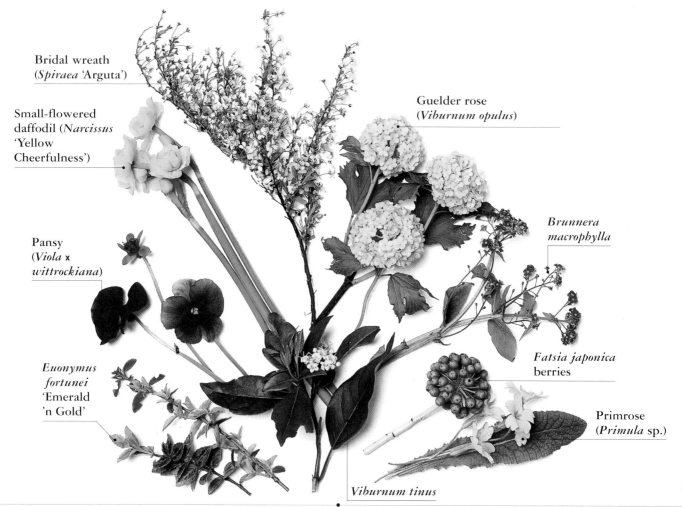

Bridal wreath (*Spiraea* 'Arguta')

Small-flowered daffodil (*Narcissus* 'Yellow Cheerfulness')

Guelder rose (*Viburnum opulus*)

Brunnera macrophylla

Pansy (*Viola* x *wittrockiana*)

Fatsia japonica berries

Euonymus fortunei 'Emerald 'n Gold'

Primrose (*Primula* sp.)

Viburnum tinus

Making the base

Cover the central cavity of the oasis ring with cardboard or aluminium foil
to make a good base for the "nest" in the centre of the arrangement.

1 *Soak the oasis ring in water for at least half an hour, then
leave to drain. Place the ring on a sheet of cardboard or
aluminium foil, and draw a circle around its outer edge.*

2 *Cut out the cardboard or aluminium foil circle, cutting 2 cm
(¾ in) inside the mark. Attach the cut circle to the base of the
oasis ring with florist's tape.*

Step-by-step arranging

See also: Foundations (pp. 20–21); Flower and leaf shape (pp. 46–7); Round
arrangements (pp. 48–9); Textural effects (pp. 92–3).

1 *Separate the viburnum tinus into sprigs of flowers and leaves,
removing the lower leaves. Push the flower sprigs into the ring
in three groups, spacing them evenly around the base.*

2 *Place viburnum leaves on the sides of the ring by pushing them
into the outer edge so that they fan out around it to make an
asymmetrical frame.*

3 *Insert small groups of variegated
euonymus leaves in the ring at evenly
spaced intervals. These provide a contrast to
the dark leaves of viburnum.*

4 *Group the daffodils into bunches of
5–6, and space them evenly around the
ring. These add a different form and colour
to the arrangement.*

5 *Insert the delicate, round-headed
guelder roses in the ring, positioning
them close to the daffodils.*

VARIATION

*Similar textures, but a different colour palette, have been used for this
autumn variation with its bronze, gold and green tints. A selection of nuts
could be placed in the centre of the arrangement in place of the eggs.*

Golden rod
(**Solidago** sp.)

Privet
(**Ligustrum** sp.)

Hypericum berries

Spray chrysanthemum
(**Chrysanthemum** sp.)

Spray chrysanthemum
(**Chrysanthemum** sp.)

Viburnum tinus

Ivy (**Hedera** sp.)

Hydrangea
(**Hydrangea** sp.)

Pyracantha berries
(**Pyracantha** sp.)

6 *Space the fatsia japonica berries at equal intervals around the ring and on the sides.*

7 *Punch four holes at regular intervals around the ring with the pointed end of a biro or pencil. Insert tiny bunches of primroses into these holes.*

8 *Repeat Step 7 using the pansies. Fill in gaps with white bridal wreath and blue brunnera. Fill the centre of the ring with moss, and arrange the eggs on top.*

Scent

INVISIBLE TO THE EYE, scent is nevertheless a valuable ingredient that gives an extra dimension to any flower arrangement. This chapter pictures a variety of fragrant flowers and aromatic herbs that both look and smell good and discusses how best to include them in an aromatic display. The perfumes explored range from the spiciness of herbs, through the sweet perfume of lilac, to the heady fragrance of hyacinths.

Scented Plants

SCENT IS A QUALITY found in both flowers and foliage. Scents are difficult to describe and vary enormously, from the heady sweetness of hyacinths to the pleasantly sharp smell of wormwood. The plants shown here are ideal for flower arranging as they are both attractive and fragrantly scented. Whether or not you find a particular scent attractive is a entirely a matter of personal taste, but if you are planning to use several scented plants in an arrangement, make sure that the fragrances do not clash and cancel each other out.

Lilac
(*Syringa* sp.)

'Star Gazer' lily
(*Lilium speciosum*
'Star Gazer')

Broom
(*Genista* sp.)

Freesia
(*Freesia* sp.)

Rose
(*Rosa* 'Fritz Nobis')

Rose
(*Rosa rugosa* 'Alba')

Rose
(*Rosa* 'Etoile
de Hollande')

Rose
(*Rosa* 'Gloire
de Dijon')

Rose
(*Rosa* 'Blessings')

Hyacinth
(*Hyacinthus* sp.)

Small-flowering
daffodil (*Narcissus* sp.)

Mimosa
(*Acacia* sp.)

Christmas box
(*Sarcococca
hookeriana*)

Florist's rose
(*Rosa* sp.)

Geranium
(*Pelargonium* sp.)

Viburnum tinus

*Pelargonium
graveolens*
'Lady Plymouth'

Easter lily
(*Lilium
longiflorum*)

Wormwood
(*Artemisia* sp.)

Crab apple
(*Malus* sp.)

Common myrtle
(*Myrtus communis*)

Mexican
orange
blossom
(*Choisya
ternata*)

Sweet pea
(*Lathyrus odoratus*)

Carnation
(*Dianthus* sp.)

Honeysuckle
(*Lonicera* sp.)

Aromatic Herbs

VALUED FOR CENTURIES for their aromatic and healing properties, herbs make a wonderful contribution to flower arrangements, either grouped together in an old-fashioned posy, or combined with other flowers to add scent and spice to an arrangement. Here is a selection of some popular and useful herbs. When using herbs in an arrangement, be sure to condition them first (see page 22), as the soft-stemmed forms are inclined to wilt rapidly.

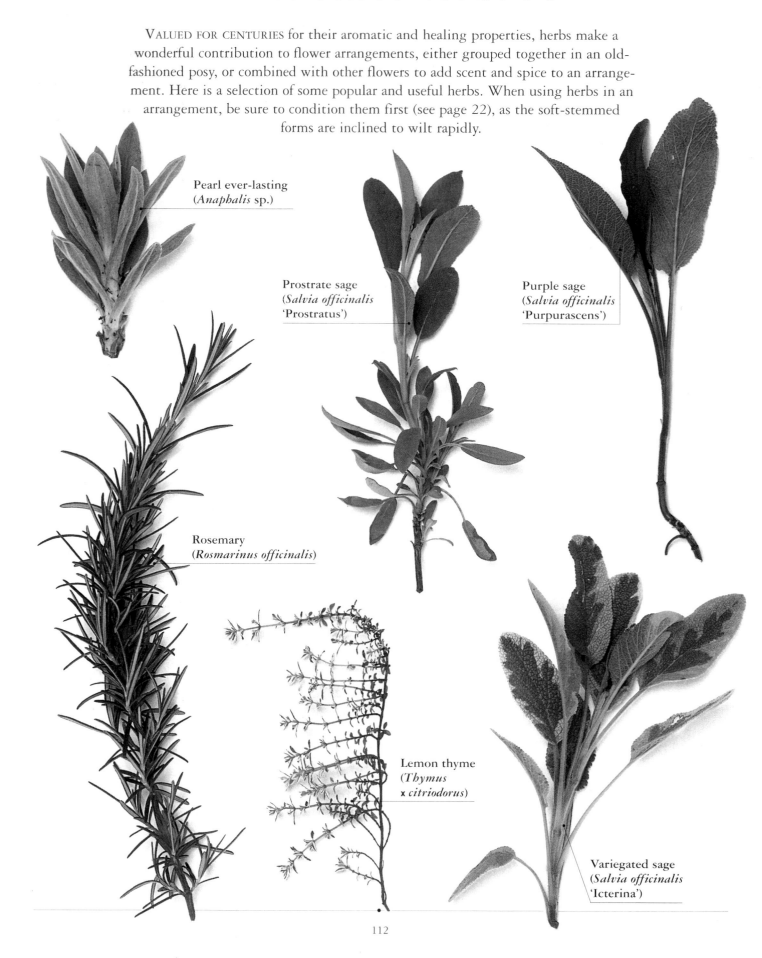

Pearl ever-lasting
(*Anaphalis* sp.)

Prostrate sage
(*Salvia officinalis*
'Prostratus')

Purple sage
(*Salvia officinalis*
'Purpurascens')

Rosemary
(*Rosmarinus officinalis*)

Lemon thyme
(*Thymus*
x *citriodorus*)

Variegated sage
(*Salvia officinalis*
'Icterina')

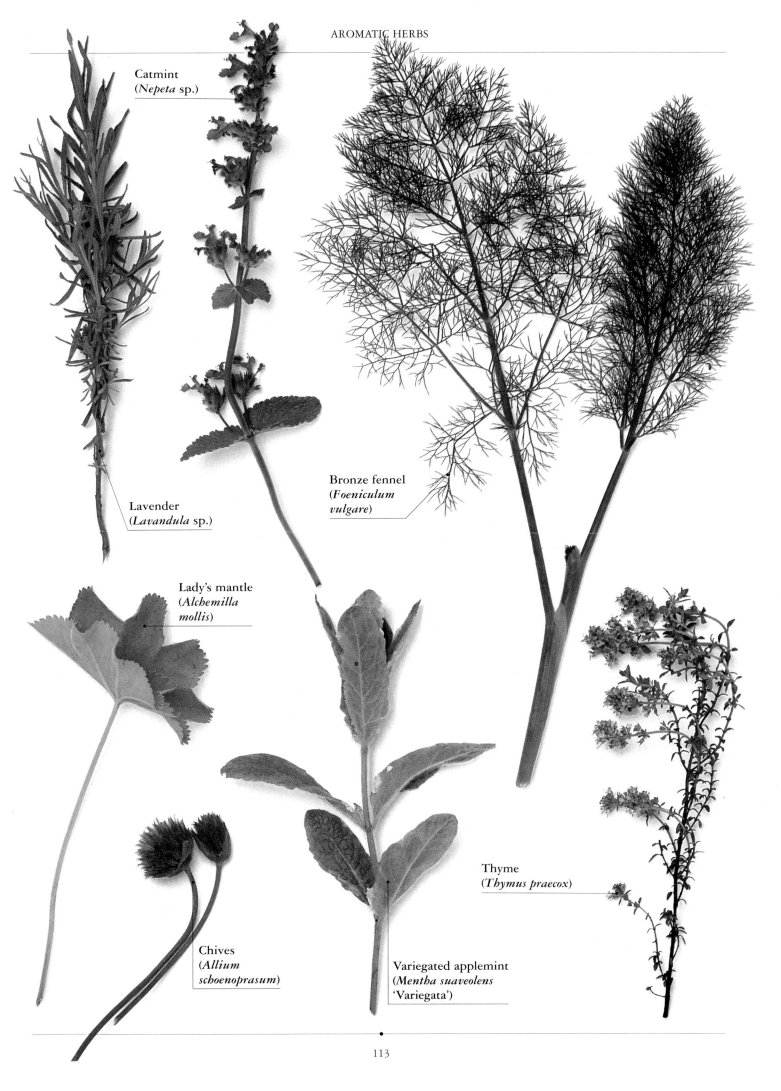

Catmint
(*Nepeta* sp.)

Lavender
(*Lavandula* sp.)

Bronze fennel
(*Foeniculum vulgare*)

Lady's mantle
(*Alchemilla mollis*)

Thyme
(*Thymus praecox*)

Chives
(*Allium schoenoprasum*)

Variegated applemint
(*Mentha suaveolens* 'Variegata')

Sweet and Light:
Lilac Blossom Pitcher

MATERIALS

30-cm (12-in) length
chicken wire

Large ceramic pitcher

6–8 branched stems lilac
(*Syringa vulgaris*)

3–4 branched stems Mexican
orange blossom (*Choisya ternata*)

6–8 stems cow parsley
(*Anthriscus sylvestris*)

3–4 stems pink cherry blossom
(*Prunus* sp.)

7 white tulips (*Tulipa*
'White Triumphator')

WITH ITS INSTANTLY recognisable, heady smell, lilac is one of the most popular scented plants to bring into the house. It tends to look best in simple, informal arrangements, where its naturally gnarled branches can provide the basic shape for the display. When combining lilac with other flowers, make sure it is not overwhelmed by them. Wild or informal-looking flowers, such as the cow parsley, cherry blossom, Mexican orange blossom and lily-flowered tulips used in this arrangement, harmonise well with it; but large, artificially induced florist's flowers would make too bold a statement and detract from the main ingredient. Here, glossy green leaves of Mexican orange blossom are included for textural and tonal contrast and to give the arrangement more substance.

RIGHT: *The chief attribute of this arrangement is the scent, which comes principally from the lilac, but also from the Mexican orange blossom. The soft, harmonising colours, combined with the small, delicate flowers, unite the arrangement.*

Tulip
(*Tulipa* 'WhiteTriumphator')

Mexican orange blossom
(*Choisya ternata*)

Lilac
(*Syringa vulgaris*)

Cow parsley
(*Anthriscus sylvestris*)

Cherry blossom
(*Prunus* sp.)

Preparing the materials

With a deep, narrow-necked container such as this one, you can sometimes dispense with any anchoring material, but, because lilac stems tend to be twisted, inserting a ball of chicken wire into the base of the container makes it easier to keep them in place.

1 *Crumple the chicken wire into a ball shape and insert it into the pitcher to provide the foundation for the arrangement. Fill the pitcher three-quarters full with fresh, cold water.*

2 *Cut the stems of the flowers to size: the tallest branches should be roughly twice the height of the container. Strip away the lower leaves below the water line. Crush the stems with a hammer.*

Step-by-step arranging

See also: Foundations (pp. 20–21); Conditioning flowers (pp. 22–3); Importance of natural shapes (pp. 32–3); Textural effects (pp. 92–3); Scented plants (pp.110–111).

1 *Place the lilac and the Mexican orange blossom in the pitcher, following a rounded outline and allowing the lilac to arch naturally. This forms the framework for the arrangement.*

2 *Using smaller branches of lilac and Mexican orange blossom, fill in the overall rounded shape. Occasionally drape a sprig over the side of the pitcher.*

VARIATION

*This is a richer, darker autumn variation on the lilac pitcher, with lilies forming the
scented element. Glowing golds, reds and deep glossy greens marry well together,
with the paler flowers adding a touch of light.*

Montbretia seedheads
(*Crocosmia* sp.)

Viburnum tinus
leaves and berries

September flower
(*Aster* sp.)

Lily
(*Lilium* sp.)

Spray chrysanthemum
(*Chrysanthemum* sp.)

Goldenrod
(*Solidago* sp.)

3 *Insert the stems of cow parsley at the back of the arrangement,
interspersing them with the tall sprigs of cherry blossom.
This prevents the arrangement from looking overly symmetrical form
and enhances its natural feel.*

4 *Place white tulips in any gaps. The tulips are such a strong
shape that they could dominate, but being white, they only give
an attractive finishing touch.*

Strong and Heady: Spring Miscellany

MATERIALS

45-cm (18-in) square chicken wire

Reel wire

Shallow bowl, 30 cm (12 in) in diameter

Vine wreath base

Cling film

Moss

3–4 blue hyacinths (*Hyacinthus* sp.)

16 grape hyyacinths (*Muscari* sp.)

1 pot yellow primroses (*Primula* sp.)

4 sprigs variegated ivy (*Hedera helix*)

2 large sprigs tree ivy (*Hedera helix* 'Arborea')

24 small-flowered daffodils (*Narcissus* 'Soleil d'Or')

T HE LARGEST PROFUSION of scented flowers occurs in spring, and ranges from the delicate scent of primroses to the heady perfume of hyacinths. This small spring garden provides a mixture of different scents. The grape hyacinths have no fragrance, but they provide a structural link between the large cylinder-shaped hyacinths and the flatter, open petals of the primroses. The blue and yellow colours chosen are common to many spring bulbs. The flowers are arranged to echo the way bulbs grow naturally in the garden, with the hyacinths providing the height. This arrangement would make an attractive decoration for a low coffee table or a display in a window embrasure. Because primroses are notoriously short-lived when picked and placed in water, the primroses used here are container-grown to provide a longer-lasting display. This arrangement can also be made using entirely pot-grown plants, with moss covering the pots to disguise them.

RIGHT: *The plants are arranged according to their natural scale to produce a highly scented and charming spring "garden". Strong visual interest is created by using flowers of differing forms.*

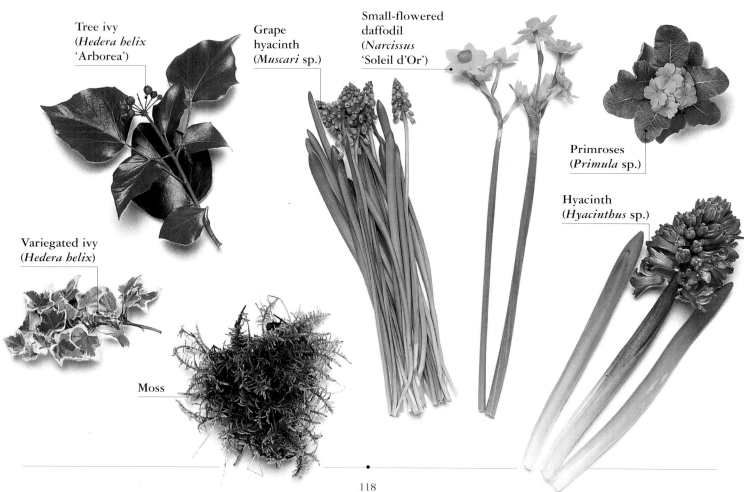

Tree ivy (*Hedera helix* 'Arborea')

Grape hyacinth (*Muscari* sp.)

Small-flowered daffodil (*Narcissus* 'Soleil d'Or')

Primroses (*Primula* sp.)

Hyacinth (*Hyacinthus* sp.)

Variegated ivy (*Hedera helix*)

Moss

Making the base

For this base, a shallow bowl is filled with scrunched chicken wire, covered with moss, and surrounded by a vine wreath. Alternatively, you could use a wide, shallow wicker basket and line it with plastic.

1 *Scrunch the chicken wire. Attach reel wire to one side of the chicken wire and take it under the bowl. Fasten it to the opposite side of the chicken wire. Repeat, crossing the reel wire under the bowl.*

2 *Place the bowl in the centre of the vine wreath base. Fill the bowl with fresh, cool water.*

3 *Loosely cover the surface of the chicken wire and the sides of the vine wreath base with pieces of moss.*

Step-by-step arranging

See also: Foundations (pp. 20–21); Round arrangements (pp. 48–9); Yellows and oranges (pp. 68–9); Mauves and blues (pp. 72–3); Scented plants (pp. 110–111).

1 *Secure the hyacinth leaves to the flower stems with an elastic band. The hyacinths are inserted into the moss-covered bowl first to form a framework for the rest of the arrangement.*

2 *Insert the hyacinths in the centre of the arrangement, pushing them down firmly. Bunch 6 stems of grape hyacinths together and insert close to the hyacinths.*

3 *Remove the primroses from their pot. Gently shake off any loose soil, and wrap the root ball in cling film.*

4 At one side of the dish, cut a hole in the chicken wire to form a space for the wrapped primrose pot. Carefully mould the chicken wire around the pot with your fingers in order to hold it upright, taking care not to disturb any of the other elements of the arrangement as you do so.

5 Drape the sprigs of both the tree ivy and the variegated ivy across the rim of the vine wreath base. This makes the whole arrangement look as if it is growing out of the ground, like a tiny woodland garden.

6 Make 3–4 bunches of daffodils with about 6 stems in each one, and tie them together with elastic bands. (Take care not to tie them too tightly or you will break the stems.) Space the bunches at intervals around the arrangement.

7 Check that the plants are regularly spaced throughout the arrangement and that the overall shape is a rounded dome. Keep the tallest flowers in the centre, and fill in any gaps with the remaining flowers and foliage.

Spicy and Musky: Herb Bowl

MATERIALS

30-cm (12-in) square of
5-cm (2-in) chicken wire

Shallow bowl, 25 cm
(10 in) in diameter

8 stems pearl everlasting
(*Anaphalis* sp.)

5 sprigs purple sage (*Salvia
officinalis* 'Purpurascens')

8 sprigs variegated apple
mint (*Mentha suaveolens*
'Variegata')

6–7 stems lady's mantle
(*Alchemilla mollis*)

6 stems deadnettle (*Lamium* sp.)

6 sprigs curly mint
(*Mentha spicata* 'Crispii')

6 sprigs geranium
(*Pelargonium graveolens*
'Lady Plymouth')

15 stems lavender (*Lavandula
angustifolia* 'Hidcote')

THIS SMALL BOWL contains a nosegay of aromatic herbs along with a few other foliage plants to add substance. You can use any herbs, but be sure to include some highly fragrant ones such as lavender, scented geraniums or thyme. The scents of different herbs have remarkable therapeutic properties: lavender is generally regarded as calming, rosemary as invigorating, for example. A scented herb arrangement gives any room a welcoming feel.

When making an arrangement of herbs, limit the colour palette for greatest effect; here soft greens, mauves and pinks were used. Equally attractive colour combinations would be silver-leafed herbs, such as rosemary, artemisia, thyme and lavender, combined with blue and mauve flowers, or a white-and-green combination with feverfew flowers, white roses, lady's mantle and variegated foliage.

This arrangement is made by using a simple chicken-wire base to hold the stems. Insert the herbs in bunches; this will make the arrangement look much more solid than if you inserted the stems individually.

RIGHT: *This arrangement relies on a sweet and musky base scent (lavender, purple sage and scented geranium leaves) combined with the lighter, fresher perfume of curly mint and apple mint. Never include too many scents in the same arrangement or they will counteract each other.*

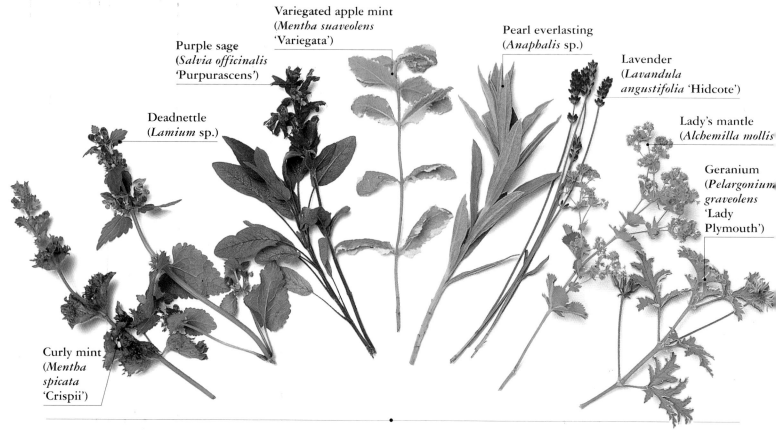

Variegated apple mint
(*Mentha suaveolens*
'Variegata')

Purple sage
(*Salvia officinalis*
'Purpurascens')

Pearl everlasting
(*Anaphalis* sp.)

Lavender
(*Lavandula
angustifolia* 'Hidcote')

Deadnettle
(*Lamium* sp.)

Lady's mantle
(*Alchemilla mollis*

Geranium
(*Pelargonium
graveolens*
'Lady
Plymouth')

Curly mint
(*Mentha
spicata*
'Crispii')

Step-by-step arranging

See also: Foundations (pp. 20–21); Conditioning flowers (pp. 22–3); Round
arrangements (pp. 48–9); Aromatic herbs (pp. 112–113).

1 *Stretch the chicken wire over the bowl,
bending it over the lip. Alternatively,
secure the chicken wire with reel wire (see
page 120). Fill with water.*

2 *Remove the lower leaves of the pearl
everlasting. Trim them to 10 cm (4 in)
above the bowl's rim. Place them round the
edge of the bowl to form a collar.*

3 *Trim the purple sage as in Step 2,
removing the lower leaves if necessary.
Insert the sage in the spaces between the
pearl everlasting.*

4 *Divide the variegated apple mint into three groups of two
stems each. Place them at regular intervals between the pearl
everlasting and the purple sage.*

5 *Take six or seven stems of lady's mantle and bunch them
together, securing them with a rubber band. Insert the bunch
in the centre of the arrangement so that it stands higher than the
surrounding herbs.*

VARIATION

A lighter and sweeter, though still fairly aromatic, combination can be made by arranging lady's mantle with purple sage and pale pink, scented garden roses.

Lady's mantle
(*Alchemilla mollis*)

Rose
('*Rosa* 'New Dawn')

Purple sage
(*Salvia officinalis* 'Purpurascens')

6 Group the deadnettle into two bunches of three stems. Place them between the lady's mantle and the outer collar of pearl everlasting.

7 Group the curly mint into two bunches of three stems each. Insert each bunch where it provides best contrast with the paler pearl everlasting.

8 Insert geranium leaves in any spaces. Insert lavender in the centre, easing it between the stems of lady's mantle. Fill any remaining gaps with pearl everlasting.

Index

A

Abies, 99
Acacia, 69, 111
  A. dealbata, 32
Achillea, 10
Aconitum, 73
Adhesive tape, 21
Adiantum, 47
Aegopodium, 36, 37
Air locks, removing, 23
Ajuga, 73
Alchemilla mollis, 36, 68, 94, 113, 122–125
Alder, 41
Alexandrian laurel, 35
Alkanet, 42
Allium, 66
  A. aflatunense, 43, 46, 72
  A. schoenoprasum, 70, 113
Alnus, 41
Alstroemeria, 69, 70, 85, 89
Amaryllis, 32, 48
Anaphalis, 95, 112, 122–124
Anemones, 24, 67, 70, 72, 74–76, 93, 99
Anethum graveolens, 10, 48, 82–84, 85
Anthriscus sylvestris, 42, 67, 114–116
Antirrhinum, 43
Apple blossom, 77
Applemint, 92, 113, 122–124
Aquilegia, 36, 71, 86–88
Artemisia, 111
Aster, 10, 63, 117
Astrantia, 36, 37, 47
Autumn Basket, 78–81
Autumn Centrepiece, 56–59

B

Ballota, 92
Baskets, 17, 78–81
Begonia, 56–58
Bergenia, 56–58, 93
Betula, 10, 94
Birch catkins, 94
Birch twigs, 10
Blue pine, 99
Bluebells, 73, 77
Blue flowers, 72–73
Bouquets, 26
Bows, 28–29
Box, 47, 94
Bridal wreath, 67, 104–106
Brilliant Summer Vase, 86–89

Broom, 95, 110
Brunnera macrophylla, 73, 74–76, 104–106
Buds, opening, 25
Bugle, 73
Buttercups, 10, 32, 33, 42
Buxus sempervirens, 47, 94

C

Calendula, 10, 78–80, 81
  C. officinalis, 86–88, 89
Camellias, 71, 95
Campions, 32, 37, 40, 42, 63, 67, 70
Carnations, 10, 32, 34–35, 69, 111
Carpinus, 37, 82–84
Catmint, 73, 113
Cellophane, bouquets, 26
Centaurea, 10
Centrepieces, 56–59, 104–107
Chamaecyparis lawsoniana, 41, 96–98
Chamaedaphne calyculata, 41
Cherry blossom, 114–116
Chicken wire, 15, 20
Chincherinchee, 85
Chinese lanterns, 41
Chives, 70, 113
Choisya ternata, 36, 77, 92, 93, 111, 114–116
Christmas box, 95, 111
Chrysanthemum, 10, 32, 38, 39, 66, 69, 78–80, 96–98, 103, 107, 117
  C. parthenium, 68, 95
Clashing colours, 86–89
Clematis, 10, 46
  C. 'Arabella', 72
  C. 'Wada's Primrose', 82–84
Colour, 65–89
Columbines, 71, 86–88
Comfrey, 66, 74–76, 85
Conditioning flowers, 22–23
Containers, 16–19, 38–39
Convolvulus cneorum, 67
Cool colours, 74–77
Cornflowers, 10
Cornus, 10, 60–62, 96–98
  C. alba 'Elegantissima', 37, 43, 63
  C.a. 'Spaethii', 68
Corsican hellebore, 66
Corylus, 94
Cotinus coggygria, 63
Cow parsley, 32, 42, 67, 114–116

Crab apple blossom, 111
Cranesbills, 40, 73
Crocosmia, 117
Cymbidium, 55

D

Daffodils, 10, 32, 68, 81, 100–102, 104–106, 111, 118–121
Danäe racemosa, 35
Daylilies, 69
Dead flower heads, removing, 23
Deadnettle, 72, 122–124
Delphinium, 10, 43
  D. belladonna 'Blue Bees', 73
Design principles, 31–43
Dianthus, 10, 69, 111
Dill, 10, 48, 82–84, 85
Dogwood, 10, 37, 43, 60–62, 63, 68, 96–98
Dome-shaped arrangements, 56–59

E

Easter Centrepiece, 104–107
Easter lily, 63, 111
Equipment, 14-15
Eucalyptus, 10, 38, 50, 85, 95
Euonymus, 36
  E. fortunei 'Emerald 'n Gold', 37, 43, 50, 68, 78–81, 104–106
Euphorbia, 10, 23
  E. amygdaloides, 63
  E. polychroma, 36, 37, 59, 82–84
Eustoma, 63
  E. grandiflorum, 43, 46, 66, 71, 89

F

Facing arrangements, 50–51, 60–63
Fatsia japonica, 10, 46, 93, 104–106
Fennel, 113
Ferns, 92
Feverfew, 68, 95
Florist's tape, 14
Florist's wire, 14
Foeniculum vulgare, 113
Foliage. *See* leaves

Forsythia x *intermedia* 'Spectabilis', 69
Foundations, 15, 20–21
Freesias, 10, 24, 50, 66, 110
'Frogs', 15
Fruit, 56–59

G

Galanthus nivalis, 10
  G.n. 'Flore plena', 66
Genista, 95, 110
Geranium, 40, 46, 67, 70, 71, 111, 122–124
  G. 'Johnson's Blue', 40, 73
  G. phaeum 'Alba', 66
Gerbera, 24, 43, 50, 86–88, 99
Ginger heliconia, 43
Gladioli, 10, 24
Gloriosa superba, 86–89
Glory lily, 86–89
Golden rod, 36, 50, 107, 117
Grape hyacinths, 10, 46, 118–121
Grasses, 42, 92
Green flowers, 66–67
Ground elder, 36, 37
Guelder rose, 36, 46, 48, 67, 104–106

H

Hazel catkins, 94
Hebe, 94
  H. pinguifolia, 67
Hedera, 10, 36, 37, 41, 47, 55, 92, 99, 107
  H. helix, 118–121
  H.h. 'Arborea', 93, 118–121
  H. hibernica 'Deltoidea', 67
Helianthus, 69
Heliconia, 43
Helleborus, 10, 36, 47
  H. argutifolius, 66
  H. foetidus, 66
  H. x *hybridus*, 52–54, 71
  H. orientalis, 66
Hemerocallis, 69
Herb Bowl, 122–124
Herbs, 112–113
Heuchera 'Palace Purple', 52–55
Hippeastrum, 48
Holly, 10, 36, 60–62, 94, 96–99
Honesty, 10, 46
Honeysuckle, 111

Hornbeam, 37, 82–84
Hosta, 10, 36, 43, 47, 63
  H. fortunei, 37, 82–84
  H.f. 'Aurea Marginata',
    82–84
  H. 'Golden Sunburst', 59
Hyacinthoides non-scripta, 73, 77
Hyacinthus, 71, 73, 94, 110,
  118–121
  H. orientalis, 73
Hydrangea, 107
  H. anomala subsp. *petiolaris*,
    37
Hypericum, 107

I

Ilex, 10, 36, 60–62, 96–99
  I. aquifolium, 94
Iris, 10, 24, 46, 47, 73,
  77, 89, 93
  I. japonica, 37
Ivy, 10, 36, 37, 41, 47, 55, 67,
  92, 93, 99, 107, 118–121
Ivy-leafed geranium, 40

K

Knives, 14

L

Lady's mantle, 68, 94, 113,
  122–125
Lamb's tongue, 67, 92
Lamium, 122–124
  L. maculatum, 72
Larch, 41, 99
Larix, 41, 99
Larkspur, 24
Lathyrus odoratus, 10, 66, 70,
  72, 111
Lavandula (lavender), 10, 46,
  113, 122–124
  L. angustifolia 'Hidcote', 46,
    122–124
Lawson's cypress, 41, 96–98
Leatherleaf, 41
Leaves, 34–37
  leafy containers, 18
  removing, 22, 25
  shapes, 47
Lemon thyme, 37, 112
Leptospermum, 48, 71
Lettuce, 52–54
Ligustrum, 35, 107
Lilac, 10, 46, 66, 67, 72, 95,
  110, 114–116
Lilac Blossom Pitcher,
  114–116
Lilium (lilies), 6, 10, 23, 32,

43, 59, 69, 85, 86–89,
  117
L. 'Journey's End', 56–58
L. longiflorum, 63, 111
L. speciosum 'Star Gazer', 43,
  110
Limited palette, 82–85
Lisianthus, 6, 43, 46, 63, 66,
  71, 89
Lonicera, 111
Low arrangements, 52–55
Lunaria, 10
  L. annua, 46

M

Magnolia grandiflora, 60–62, 92
Mahonia, 10, 46, 60–62, 93,
  94, 96–98
  M. aquifolium, 40, 69
Maidenhair fern, 47
Malus, 77, 111
Marbles, 15, 21
Marigolds, 10, 24, 78–80, 81,
  86–88, 89
Matthiola, 10, 40, 43, 50, 68,
  86–89
  M. incana, 66
Mauve flowers, 72–73
Meadow rue, 47, 72
Melaleuca, 41
Mentha spicata 'Crispii', 92,
  122–124
  M. suaveolens 'Variegata', 92,
    113, 122–124
Mexican orange blossom, 77,
  92, 93, 111, 114–116
Mimosa, 32, 69, 111
Mint, 92, 122–124
Monkshood, 73
Montbretia, 117
Moss, 19, 78–80, 100–102,
  118–121
Muscari, 10, 46, 118–121
Myrtle, 111
Myrtus communis, 111

N

Narcissus, 10, 81, 111
  N. 'February Gold', 68
  N. 'Soleil d'Or', 100–102,
    118–121
  N. tazetta, 68
  N. 'Tête-à-Tête', 68
  N. 'Yellow Cheerfulness',
    104–106
Nepeta, 113
  N. x *faassenii*, 73
  N. nervosa, 73
Nerine, 10
  N. bowdenii, 56–58

O

Oasis, 15, 20
Oasis pins, 14
Oasis tape, 14
Onions, 66, 72
Orange flowers, 68–69
Orchids, 55, 60–62, 70, 94
Ornithogalum thyrsoides, 85

P

Pansies, 10, 37, 40, 73, 77, 93,
  104–106
Pearl everlasting, 95, 112,
  122–124
Pelargonium, 40, 46, 67, 71, 111
  P. 'Cascade', 70
  P. graveolens 'Lady Plymouth',
    111, 122–124
  P. 'Royal Ascot', 70
Pentaglottis sempervirens, 42
Peonies, 10, 43, 71, 86–88
Petals, damaged, 25
Phlox 'Chatahoochee', 72
Physalis, 41
Pine cones, 99
Pink flowers, 70–71
Pins, 14
Pinus, 99
Pittosporum, 41
Polyanthus, 10, 68, 72
Polypodium vulgare, 92
Posies, 27
Preparing flowers, 24–25
Primroses, 10, 104–106,
  118–121
Primula, 41, 68, 72, 104–106,
  118–121
  P. 'Captain Blood', 70
Privet, 35, 107
Protea, 41
Prunus, 114–116
Pteris cretica, 47
Pussy willow, 93
Pyracantha, 10, 107
  P. coccinea, 41

Q

Queen Anne's lace, 6

R

Raffia, 14
Ranunculus, 10, 33, 42
  R. asiaticus, 68, 70, 85, 93
Red flowers, 70–71
Reel wire, 14
Ribbon fern, 47

Ribbons, 14
  bows, 28–29
Rope, 14
Rosa (roses), 10, 24, 25, 32, 43,
  69, 85, 86–89, 92, 111
  R. 'Blessings', 110
  R. 'Bridal Pink', 48
  R. 'Céleste', 40
  R. de Meaux, 71
  R. 'Etoile de Hollande', 70,
    110
  R. 'Fritz Nobis', 110
  R. glauca, 70
  R. 'Gloire de Dijon', 40, 110
  R. 'Maigold', 68, 82–84
  R. 'New Dawn', 46, 125
  R. 'Nicole', 60–62
  R. rugosa 'Alba', 67, 110
Rosmarinus officinalis (rosemary),
  36, 37, 72, 94, 112
Round arrangements, 48–49,
  52–59
Rubber bands, 14

S

Sage, 47, 94, 112, 122–125
Salix, 71, 93
Salvia nemorosa, 40
  S. officinalis, 47
  S.o. 'Icterina', 112
  S.o. 'Prostratus', 112
  S.o. 'Purpurascens', 94, 112,
    122–124, 125
Saponaria, 34
Sarcococca hookeriana, 95, 111
Scent, 109–125
Scissors, 14
Senecio, 35, 36
  S. laxifolius, 10, 48, 92, 95
  S. 'Sunshine', 40, 74–76, 85
September flowers, 10, 63, 117
Shape, 45–63
  containers, 38–39
  flowers, 32–33, 46
  leaves, 47
Silene dioica, 42, 70
  S. fimbriata, 37, 40, 42, 63,
    67
Singapore orchids, 60–62, 70,
  94
Singeing stems, 23
Skimmia, 93, 94
  S. japonica, 70
  S. rubella, 93, 94
Snapdragons, 43
Snowdrops, 10, 66
Solidago, 36, 107, 117
  S. canadensis, 50
Spiraea, 10, 35, 47
  S. 'Arguta', 67, 104–106
Spring Bowl, 74–77
Spring Hellebore Dish, 52–55

Spring Miscellany, 118–121
Spring Narcissi Pots, 100–102
Stachys byzantina, 36, 37, 67, 92
Stamens, removing, 23
Stems: crushing, 22
  singeing, 23
  straightening, 24
  wiring, 25
Stinking hellebore, 66
Stocks, 10, 40, 43, 50, 66, 68, 86–89
Straightening stems, 24
String, 14
Summer Jug, 82–85
Sunflowers, 69
Sweet peas, 10, 66, 70, 72, 111
Symphytum, 85
  S. grandiflorum, 66, 74–76
Syringa, 10, 46, 66, 67, 72, 95, 110
  S. vulgaris, 114–116

T

Taxus baccata, 96–98
Tazetta narcissus, 68
Techniques, 13–19
Teucrium fruticans, 47
Texture, 36, 91–107
Thalictrum, 47, 72
Thorns, 24, 25
Thymus (thyme), 113
  T. x *citriodorus*, 37, 112
  T. praecox, 113
Tolmiea, 37
  T. menziesii, 82–84
Trachelium, 89
  T. caeruleum, 43, 50, 72
Tulipa (tulips), 10, 24, 25, 32, 33, 48, 66, 71, 77, 93
  T. 'White Triumphator', 114–116

V

Vaccaria hispanica, 34
Viburnum, 10
  V. opulus, 36, 46, 48, 67, 104–106
  V. tinus, 36, 67, 77, 104–107, 111, 117
Viola, 10, 37, 40, 77
  V. x *wittrockiana*, 73, 93, 104–106

W

Warm colours, 78–81
Water, 22
White flowers, 66–67
Willow, 71
Winter Bucket, 96–99

Wire, 14
Wiring stems, 25
Wood spurge, 63
Wormwood, 111
Wreath bases, 15

Y

Yellow flowers, 68–69
Yew, 96–98

Acknowledgements

Jenny Raworth and Susan Berry would like to thank the following people
for all their hard work in helping to create this book:

Mike Newton, assisted by Richard Smith, for his excellent photography;
Art Director Roger Bristow; Kevin Williams and Carol McCleeve for designing the book;
Sarah Hoggett and Catherine Ward for their editorial work,
assisted by Deirdre Mitchell and Corinne Asghar;
Production Director Kate MacPhee; Marketing Assistant Suzi Elsden;
Brian Mathew for checking plant names; and
Hilary Bird for compiling the index.

Thanks also to Jill and Jenny at Broadway Flower Shop
and to Lavenders of London for supplying
flowers and other materials.